Forbidden Fruit

ABELARD AND HELOISE

Forbidden Fruit

from the Letters of Abelard and Heloise

Translated by BETTY RADICE
Revised by M. T. CLANCHY

GREAT 🐧🐧 LOVES

PENGUIN BOOKS

Published by the Penguin Group
Penguin Books Ltd, 80 Strand, London WC2R ORL, England
Penguin Group (USA) Inc., 375 Hudson Street, New York, New York 10014, USA
Penguin Group (Canada), 90 Eglinton Avenue East, Suite 700, Toronto, Ontario, Canada M4P 2Y3
(a division of Pearson Penguin Canada Inc.)
Penguin Ireland, 25 St Stephen's Green, Dublin 2, Ireland
(a division of Penguin Books Ltd)
Penguin Group (Australia), 250 Camberwell Road, Camberwell, Victoria 3124, Australia
(a division of Pearson Australia Group Pty Ltd)
Penguin Books India Pvt Ltd, 11 Community Centre, Panchsheel Park, New Delhi – 110 017, India
Penguin Group (NZ), 67 Apollo Drive, Rosedale, North Shore 0632, New Zealand
(a division of Pearson New Zealand Ltd)
Penguin Books (South Africa) (Pty) Ltd, 24 Sturdee Avenue,
Rosebank, Johannesburg 2196, South Africa

Penguin Books Ltd, Registered Offices: 80 Strand, London WC2R ORL, England

www.penguin.com

The Letters of Abelard and Heloise published in Penguin Books 1974
Revised edition published 2003
This extract published in Penguin Books 2007

1

Copyright © Betty Radice, 1974
All rights reserved

Typeset by Rowland Phototypesetting Ltd, Bury St Edmunds, Suffolk
Printed in England by Clays Ltd, St Ives plc

978-0-141-03480-5

Contents

Peter Abelard (1079–1142) was a French scholastic philosopher and the greatest logician of the twelfth century. He taught mainly in Paris where his fame attracted students from all over Europe and laid the foundations of the University of Paris. Heloise (1101–1162) was his pupil and through their impassioned writings unfolds the story of a romance, from its reckless, ecstatic beginnings through to public scandal, an enforced marriage and its devastating consequences. After the tragic end of their love affair and marriage she became a nun, and Abelard a monk in the Abbey of St Denis. He continued to teach theology, but his unorthodoxy led to open conflict with St Bernard of Clairvaux and his condemnation by the Church. His last months were spent under the protection of Peter the Venerable, and he died in a Cluniac priory. Heloise became abbess of the convent of Paraclete which Abelard founded, and was acclaimed for her learning, poetry and her music.

to thwart my plans and keep me from the place I had chosen. But among the powers in the land he had several enemies, and these men helped me to obtain my desire. I also won considerable support simply through his unconcealed jealousy. Thus my school had its start and my reputation for dialectic began to spread, with the result that the fame of my old fellow-students and even that of the master himself gradually declined and came to an end. Consequently my self-confidence rose still higher, and I made haste to transfer my school to Corbeil, a town nearer Paris, where I could embarrass him through more frequent encounters in disputation.

However, I was not there long before I fell ill through overwork and was obliged to return home. For some years, being remote from France, I was sought out more ardently by those eager for instruction in dialectic. A few years later, when I had long since recovered my health, my teacher William, archdeacon of Paris, changed his former status and joined the order of the Canons Regular, with the intention, it was said, of gaining promotion to a higher prelacy through a reputation for increased piety. He was soon successful when he was made bishop of Châlons. But this change in his way of life did not oblige him either to leave Paris or to give up his study of philosophy, and he soon resumed his public teaching in his usual manner in the very monastery to which he had retired to follow the religious life. I returned to him to hear his lectures on rhetoric, and in the course of our philosophic disputes I produced a sequence of clear logical arguments to make him amend, or rather abandon, his previous attitude to universals. He had maintained that in the common existence of universals, the whole species was essentially the same in each of its individuals, and among these there was no essential difference, but only variety due to multiplicity of accidents. Now he modified his view in order to say that it was the same not in essence but through non-difference. This has always been the dialectician's chief problem concerning universals, so much so that even Porphyry did not venture to settle it when he deals with universals in his *Isagoge*, but only mentioned it as a 'very serious difficulty'. Consequently, when William had modified or rather been forced to give up his original position, his lectures fell into such contempt that he was scarcely accepted on any other points of dialectic, as if the whole subject rested solely on the question of universals.

My own teaching gained so much prestige and authority from this that the strongest supporters of my master who had hitherto been the most violent among my attackers now flocked to join my school. Even William's successor as head of the Paris school offered me his chair so that he could join the others as my pupil, in the place where his master and mine had won fame. Within a few days of my taking over the teaching of dialectic, William was eaten up with jealousy and consumed with anger to an extent it is difficult to convey, and, being unable to control the violence of his resentment for long, he made another artful attempt to banish me. I had done nothing to justify his acting openly against me, so he launched an infamous attack on the man who had put me in his chair, in order to remove the school from him and put it in the hands of one of my rivals. I then returned to Melun and set up my school there as before; and the more his jealousy pursued me, the more widely my reputation spread, for, as the poet says:

Envy seeks the heights, the winds sweep the summits.

But not long after when he heard that there was considerable doubt about his piety amongst the majority of thoughtful men, and a good deal of gossip about his conversion, as it had not led to his departure from Paris, he removed himself and his little community, along with his school, to a village some distance from the city. I promptly returned to Paris from Melun, hoping for peace henceforth from him, but since he had filled my place there, as I said, by one of my rivals, I took my school outside the city to Mont-Sainte-Geneviève, and set up camp there in order to lay siege to my usurper. The news brought William back to Paris in unseemly haste to restore such scholars as remained to him and his community to their former monastery, apparently to deliver from my siege the knight whom he had abandoned. But his good intentions did the man very serious harm. He had previously had a few pupils of a sort, largely because of his lectures on Priscian, for which he had some reputation, but as soon as his master arrived he lost them all and had to retire from keeping a school. Soon afterwards he appeared to lose hope of future worldly fame, and he too was converted to the monastic life. The bouts of argument which followed William's return to the city between my pupils and him and his followers, and the successes in these battles which fortune gave my people (myself among them) are facts which you have long known. And I shall not go too far if I boldly say with Ajax that

> If you demand the issue of this fight,
> I was not vanquished by my enemy.

Should I keep silence, the facts cry out and tell the outcome.

Meanwhile my dearest mother Lucie begged me to return home, for after my father Berengar's entry into monastic life she was preparing to do the same. When she had done so I returned to France, with the special purpose of studying divinity, to find my master William (whom I have often mentioned) already installed as bishop of Châlons. However, in this field his own master, Anselm of Laon, was then the greatest authority because of his great age.

I therefore approached this old man, who owed his reputation more to long practice than to intelligence or memory. Anyone who knocked at his door to seek an answer to some question went away more uncertain than he came. Anselm could win the admiration of an audience, but he was useless when put to the question. He had a remarkable command of words but their meaning was worthless and devoid of all sense. The fire he kindled filled his house with smoke but did not light it up; he was a tree in full leaf which could be seen from afar, but on closer and more careful inspection proved to be barren. I had come to this tree to gather fruit, but I found it was the fig tree which the Lord cursed, or the ancient oak to which Lucan compares Pompey:

There stands the shadow of a noble name,
Like a tall oak in a field of corn.

Once I discovered this I did not lie idle in his shade for long. My attendance at his lectures gradually became more and more irregular, to the annoyance of some of his leading pupils, who took it as a sign of contempt for so great a master. They began secretly to turn him against me, until their base insinuations succeeded in rousing his jealousy. One day it happened that after a session of Sentences we students were joking amongst ourselves, when someone rounded on me and asked what I thought of the reading of the Holy Scriptures, when I had hitherto studied only philosophy. I replied that concentration on such reading was most beneficial for the salvation of the soul, but that I found it most surprising that for educated men the writings or glosses of the Fathers themselves were not sufficient for interpreting their commentaries without further instruction. There was general laughter, and I was asked by many of those present if I could or would venture to tackle this myself. I said I was ready to try if they wished. Still laughing, they shouted 'Right, that's settled! Take some commentary on a little-known text and we'll test what you say.' Then they all agreed on an extremely obscure prophecy of Ezekiel. I took the commentary and promptly invited them all to hear my interpretation the very next day. They then pressed unwanted advice on me, telling me not to hurry over something so important but to remember my inexperience and give longer thought to working out and confirming my exposition. I replied indignantly that it was not my custom to benefit by practice, but I relied on my own intelligence, and either they must come to my lecture at the time of my choosing or I should abandon it altogether.

At my first lecture there were certainly not many people present, for everyone thought it absurd that I could attempt this so soon, when up to now I had made no study at all of the Scriptures. But all those who came approved, so that they commended the lecture warmly, and urged me to comment on the text on the same lines as my lecture. The news brought people who had missed my first lecture flocking to the second and third ones, all alike most eager to make copies of the glosses which I had begun with on the first day.

Anselm was now wildly jealous, and being already set against me by the suggestions of some of his pupils, as I said before, he began to attack me for lecturing on the Scriptures in the same way as my master William had done previously over philosophy. There were at this time two outstanding students in the old man's school, Alberic of Rheims and Lotulf of Lombardy, whose hostility to me was intensified by the good opinion they had of themselves. It was largely through their insinuations, as was afterwards proved, that Anselm lost his head and curtly forbade me to continue my work of interpretation in the place where he taught, on the pretext that any mistake which I might write down through lack of training in the subject would be attributed to him. When this reached the ears of the students, their indignation knew no bounds – this was an act of sheer spite and calumny, such as had never been directed at anyone before; but the more open it was, the more it brought me renown, and through persecution my fame increased.

A few days after this I returned to Paris, to the school which had long ago been intended for and offered to me, and from which I had been expelled at the start. I remained in possession there in peace for several years, and as soon as I began my course of teaching I set myself to complete the commentaries on Ezekiel which I had started at Laon. These proved so popular with their readers that they judged my reputation to stand as high for my interpretation of the Scriptures as it had previously done for philosophy. The numbers in the school increased enormously as the students gathered there eager for instruction in both subjects, and the wealth and fame this brought me must be well known to you.

But success always puffs up fools with pride, and worldly security weakens the spirit's resolution and easily destroys it through carnal temptations. I began to think myself the only philosopher in the world, with nothing to fear from anyone, and so I yielded to the lusts of the flesh. Hitherto I had been entirely continent, but now the further I advanced in philosophy and theology, the further I fell behind the philosophers and holy Fathers in the impurity of my life. It is well known that the philosophers, and still more the Fathers, by which is meant those who have devoted themselves to the teachings of Holy Scripture, were especially glorified by their chastity. Since therefore I was wholly enslaved to pride and lechery, God's grace provided a remedy for both these evils, though not one of my choosing: first for my lechery by depriving me of those organs with which I practised it, and then for the pride which had grown in me through my learning – for in the words of the Apostle, 'Knowledge breeds conceit' – when I was humiliated by the burning of the book of which I was so proud.

The true story of both these episodes I now want you to know from the facts, in their proper order, instead of from hearsay. I had always held myself aloof from unclean association with prostitutes, and constant application to my studies had prevented me from frequenting the society of gentlewomen: indeed, I knew little of the secular way of life. Perverse Fortune flattered me, as the saying goes, and found an easy way to bring me toppling down from my pedestal, or rather, despite my overbearing pride and heedlessness of the grace granted me, God's compassion claimed me humbled for Himself.

There was in Paris at the time a young girl named Heloise, the niece of Fulbert, one of the canons, and so much loved by him that he had done everything in his power to advance her education in letters. In looks she did not rank lowest, while in the extent of her learning she stood supreme. A gift for letters is so rare in women that it added greatly to her charm and had made her most renowned throughout the realm. I considered all the usual attractions for a lover and decided she was the one to bring to my bed, confident that I should have an easy success; for at that time I had youth and exceptional good looks as well as my great reputation to recommend me, and feared no rebuff from any woman I might choose to honour with my love. Knowing the girl's knowledge and love of letters I thought she would be all the more ready to consent, and that even when separated we could enjoy each other's presence by exchange of written messages in which we could write many things more audaciously than we could say them, and so need never lack the pleasures of conversation.

All on fire with desire for this girl I sought an opportunity of getting to know her through private daily meetings and so more easily winning her over; and with this end in view I came to an arrangement with her uncle, with the help of some of his friends, whereby he should take me into his house, which was very near my school, for whatever sum he liked to ask. As a pretext I said that my household cares were hindering my studies and the expense was more than I could afford. Fulbert dearly loved money, and was moreover always ambitious to further his niece's education in letters, two weaknesses which made it easy for me to gain his consent and obtain my desire: he was all eagerness for my money and confident that his niece would profit from my teaching. This led him to make an urgent request which furthered my love and fell in with my wishes more than I had dared to hope; he gave me complete charge over the girl, so that I could devote all the leisure time left me by my school to teaching her by day and night, and if I found her idle I was to punish her severely. I was amazed by his simplicity – if he had entrusted a tender lamb to a ravening wolf it would not have surprised me more. In handing her over to me to punish as well as to teach, what else was he doing but giving me complete freedom to realize my desires, and providing an opportunity, even if I did not make use of it, for me to bend her to my will by threats and blows if persuasion failed? But there were two special reasons for his freedom from base suspicion: his love for his niece and my previous reputation for continence.

Need I say more? We were united, first under one roof, then in heart; and so with our lessons as a pretext we abandoned ourselves entirely to love. Her studies allowed us to withdraw in private, as love desired, and then with our books open before us, more words of love than of our reading passed between us, and more kissing than teaching. My hands strayed oftener to her bosom than to the pages; love drew our eyes to look on each other more than reading kept them on our texts. To avert suspicion I sometimes struck her, but these blows were prompted by love and tender feeling rather than anger and irritation, and were sweeter than any balm could be. In short, our desires left no stage of lovemaking untried, and if love could devise something new, we welcomed it. We entered on each joy the more eagerly for our previous inexperience, and were the less easily sated.

Now the more I was taken up with these pleasures, the less time I could give to philosophy and the less attention I paid to my school. It was utterly boring for me to have to go to the school, and equally wearisome to remain there and to spend my days on study when my nights were sleepless with lovemaking. As my interest and concentration flagged, my lectures lacked all inspiration and were merely repetitive; I could do no more than repeat what had been said long ago, and when inspiration did come to me, it was for writing love songs, not the secrets of philosophy. A lot of these songs, as you know, are still popular and sung in many places, particularly by those who enjoy the kind of life I led. But the grief and sorrow and laments of my students when they realized my preoccupation, or rather, distraction of mind are hard to realize. Few could have failed to notice something so obvious, in fact no one, I fancy, except the man whose honour was most involved – Heloise's uncle. Several people tried on more than one occasion to draw his attention to it, but he would not believe them; because, as I said, of his boundless love for his niece and my well-known reputation for chastity in my previous life. We do not easily think ill of those whom we love most, and the taint of suspicion cannot exist along with warm affection. Hence the remark of St Jerome in his letter to Sabinian: 'We are always the last to learn of evil in our own home, and the faults of our wife and children may be the talk of the town but do not reach our ears.'

But what is last to be learned is somehow learned eventually, and common knowledge cannot easily be hidden from one individual. Several months passed and then this happened in our case. Imagine the uncle's grief at the discovery, and the lovers' grief too at being separated! How I blushed with shame and contrition for the girl's plight, and what sorrow she suffered at the thought of my disgrace! All our laments were for one another's troubles, and our distress was for each other, not for ourselves. Separation drew our hearts still closer while frustration inflamed our passion even more; then we became more abandoned as we lost all sense of shame and, indeed, shame diminished as we found more opportunities for lovemaking. And so we were caught in the act as the poet says happened to Mars and Venus. Soon afterwards the girl found that she was pregnant, and immediately wrote me a letter full of rejoicing to ask what I thought she should do. One night then, when her uncle was away from home, I removed her secretly from his house, as we had planned, and sent her straight to my own country. There she stayed with my sister until she gave birth to a boy, whom she called Astralabe.

On his return her uncle went almost out of his mind – one could appreciate only by experience his transports of grief and mortification. What action could he take against me? What traps could he set? He did not know. If he killed me or did me personal injury, there was the danger that his beloved niece might suffer for it in my country. It was useless to try to seize me or confine me anywhere against my will, especially as I was very much on guard against this very thing, knowing that he would not hesitate to assault me if he had the courage or the means.

In the end I took pity on his boundless misery and went to him, accusing myself of the deceit love had made me commit as if it were the basest treachery. I begged his forgiveness and promised to make any amends he might think fit. I protested that I had done nothing unusual in the eyes of anyone who had known the power of love, and recalled how since the beginning of the human race women had brought the noblest men to ruin. Moreover, to conciliate him further, I offered him satisfaction in a form he could never have hoped for: I would marry the girl I had wronged. All I stipulated was that the marriage should be kept secret so as not to damage my reputation. He agreed, pledged his word and that of his supporters, and sealed the reconciliation I desired with a kiss. But his intention was to make it easier to betray me.

I set off at once for Brittany and brought back my friend to make her my wife. But she was strongly opposed to the proposal, and argued hotly against it for two reasons: the risk involved and the disgrace to myself. She swore that no satisfaction could ever appease her uncle, as we subsequently found out. What honour could she win, she protested, from a marriage which would dishonour me and humiliate us both? The world would justly exact punishment from her if she removed such a light from its midst. Think of the curses, the loss to the Church and grief of philosophers which would greet such a marriage! Nature had created me for all mankind – it would be a sorry scandal if I should bind myself to a single woman and submit to such base servitude. She absolutely rejected this marriage; it would be nothing but a disgrace and a burden to me. Along with the loss to my reputation she put before me the difficulties of marriage, which the apostle Paul exhorts us to avoid when he says: 'Has your marriage been dissolved? Do not seek a wife. If, however, you do marry, there is nothing wrong in it; and if a virgin marries, she has done no wrong. But those who marry will have pain and grief in this bodily life, and my aim is to spare you.' And again: 'I want you to be free from anxious care.'

But if I would accept neither the advice of the Apostle nor the exhortations of the Fathers on the heavy yoke of marriage, at least, she argued, I could listen to the philosophers, and pay regard to what had been written by them or concerning them on this subject – as for the most part the Fathers too have carefully done when they wish to rebuke us. For example, St Jerome in the first book of his *Against Jovinian* recalls how Theophrastus sets out in considerable detail the unbearable annoyances of marriage and its endless anxieties, in order to prove by the clearest possible arguments that a man should not take a wife; and he brings his reasoning from the exhortations of the philosophers to this conclusion: 'Can any Christian hear Theophrastus argue in this way without a blush?' In the same book Jerome goes on to say that 'After

Cicero had divorced Terentia and was asked by Hirtius to marry his sister he firmly refused to do so, on the grounds that he could not devote his attention to a wife and philosophy alike. He does not simply say "devote attention", but adds "alike", not wishing to do anything which would be a rival to his study of philosophy.'

But apart from the hindrances to such philosophic study, consider, she said, the true conditions for a dignified way of life. What harmony can there be between pupils and nursemaids, desks and cradles, books or tablets and distaffs, pen or stylus and spindles? Who can concentrate on thoughts of Scripture or philosophy and be able to endure babies crying, nurses soothing them with lullabies, and all the noisy coming and going of men and women about the house? Will he put up with the constant muddle and squalor which small children bring into the home? The wealthy can do so, you will say, for their mansions and large houses can provide privacy and, being rich, they do not have to count the cost nor be tormented by daily cares. But philosophers lead a very different life from rich men, and those who are concerned with wealth or are involved in mundane matters will not have time for the claims of Scripture or philosophy. Consequently, the great philosophers of the past have despised the world, not renouncing it so much as escaping from it, and have denied themselves every pleasure so as to find peace in the arms of philosophy alone. The greatest of them, Seneca, gives this advice to Lucilius: 'Philosophy is not a subject for idle moments. We must neglect everything else and concentrate on this, for no time is long enough for it. Put it aside for a moment, and you might as well give it up, for once interrupted it will not remain. We must resist all other occupations, not merely dispose of them but reject them.'

This is the practice today through love of God of those among us who truly deserve the name of monks, as it was of distinguished philosophers amongst the pagans in their pursuit of philosophy. For in every people, pagan, Jew or Christian, some men have always stood out for their faith or upright way of life, and have cut themselves off from their fellows because of their singular chastity or austerity. Amongst the Jews in times past there were the Nazirites, who dedicated themselves to the Lord according to the Law, and the sons of the prophets, followers of Elijah or Elisha, whom the Old Testament calls monks, as St Jerome bears witness; and in more recent times the three sects of philosophers described by Josephus in the eighteenth book of his *Antiquities*, the Pharisees, Sadducees and Essenes. Today we have the monks who imitate either the communal life of the apostles or the earlier, solitary life of John. Among the pagans, as I said, are the philosophers: for the name of wisdom or philosophy used to be applied not so much to acquisition of learning as to a religious way of life, as we learn from the first use of the word itself and from the testimony of the saints themselves. And so St Augustine, in the eighth book of his *City of God*, distinguishes between types of philosopher:

The Italian school was founded by Pythagoras of Samos, who is said to have been the first to use the term philosophy; before him men were called 'sages' if they seemed outstanding for some praiseworthy manner of life. But when Pythagoras was asked his profession, he replied that he was a philosopher, meaning a devotee or lover of wisdom, for he thought it too presumptuous to call himself a sage.

So the phrase 'if they seemed outstanding for some praiseworthy manner of life' clearly proves that the sages of the pagans, that is, the philosophers, were so called as a tribute to their way of life, not to their learning. There is no need for me to give examples of their chaste and sober lives – I should seem to be teaching Minerva herself. But if pagans and laymen could live in this way, though bound by no profession of religion, is there not a greater obligation on you, as clerk and canon, not to put base pleasures before your sacred duties, and to guard against being sucked down headlong into this Charybdis, there to lose all sense of shame and be plunged forever into a whirlpool of impurity? If you take no thought for the privilege of a clerk, you can at least uphold the dignity of the philosopher, and let a love of propriety curb your shamelessness if the reverence due to God means nothing to you. Remember Socrates' marriage and the sordid episode whereby he did at least remove the slur it cast on philosophy by providing an example to be a warning to his successors. This too was noted by Jerome, when he tells this tale of Socrates in the first book of his *Against Jovinian*: 'One day after he had withstood an endless stream of invective which Xanthippe poured out from a window above his head, he felt himself soaked with dirty water. All he did was to wipe his head and say: "I knew that thunderstorm would lead to rain."'

Heloise went on to the risks I should run in bringing her back, and argued that the name of friend [*amica*] instead of wife would be dearer to her and more honourable for me – only love freely given should keep me for her, not the constriction of a marriage tie, and if we had to be parted for a time, we should find the joy of being together all the sweeter the rarer our meetings were. But at last she saw that her attempts to persuade or dissuade me were making no impression on my foolish obstinacy, and she could not bear to offend me; so amidst deep sighs and tears she ended in these words: 'We shall both be destroyed. All that is left us is suffering as great as our love has been.' In this, as the whole world knows, she showed herself a true prophet.

And so when our baby son was born we entrusted him to my sister's care and returned secretly to Paris. A few days later, after a night's private vigil of prayer in a certain church, at dawn we were joined in matrimony in the presence of Fulbert and some of his, and our, friends. Afterwards we parted secretly and went our ways unobserved. Subsequently our meetings were few and furtive, in order to conceal as far as possible what we had done. But Fulbert and his household, seeking satisfaction for the dishonour done to him, began to spread the news of the marriage and break the promise of secrecy they had given me. Heloise cursed them and swore that there was no truth in this, and in his exasperation Fulbert heaped abuse on her on several occasions. As soon as I discovered this I removed her to a convent of nuns in the town near Paris called Argenteuil, where she had been brought up and educated as a small girl, and I also had made for her a religious habit of the type worn by novices, with the exception of the veil, and made her put it on.

At this news her uncle and his kinsmen and followers imagined that I had tricked them, and had found an easy way of ridding myself of Heloise by making her a nun. Wild with indignation they swore an oath against me, and one night as I slept peacefully in an inner room in my lodgings, they bribed one of my servants to admit them, and there they punished me with a most cruel and shameful vengeance of such appalling barbarity as to shock the whole world; they cut off the parts of my body whereby I had committed the wrong of which they complained. Then they fled, but the two who could be caught were blinded and castrated as I had been, one of them being the servant who had been led by greed while in my service to betray his master.

Next morning the whole city gathered before my house, and the scene of horror and amazement, mingled with lamentations, cries and groans which exasperated and distressed me, is difficult, no, impossible, to describe. In particular, the clerks and, most of all, my pupils tormented me with their unbearable weeping and wailing until I suffered more from their sympathy than from the pain of my wound, and felt the misery of my mutilation less than my shame and humiliation. All sorts of thoughts filled my mind – how brightly my reputation had shone, and now how easily in an evil moment it had been dimmed or rather completely blotted out; how just a judgement of God had struck me in the parts of the body with which I had sinned, and how just a reprisal had been taken by the very man I had myself betrayed. I thought how my rivals would exult over my fitting punishment, how this bitter blow would bring lasting grief and misery to my friends and parents, and how fast the news of this unheard-of disgrace would spread over the whole world. What road could I take now? How could I show my face in public, to be pointed at by every finger, derided by every tongue, a monstrous spectacle to all I met? I was also appalled to remember that according to the cruel letter of the Law, a eunuch is such an abomination to the Lord that men made eunuchs by the amputation or mutilation of their members are forbidden to enter a church as if they were stinking and unclean, and even animals in that state are rejected for sacrifice. 'Ye shall not present to the Lord any animal if its testicles have been bruised or crushed, torn or cut.' 'No man whose testicles have been crushed or whose organ has been severed shall become a member of the assembly of the Lord.'

I admit that it was shame and confusion in my remorse and misery rather than any devout wish for conversion which brought me to seek shelter in a monastery cloister. Heloise had already agreed to take the veil in obedience to my wishes and entered a convent.

So we both put on the religious habit, I in the abbey of St Denis, and she in the convent of Argenteuil which I spoke of before. There were many people, I remember, who in pity for her youth tried to dissuade her from submitting to the yoke of monastic rule as a penance too hard to bear, but all in vain; she broke out as best she could through her tears and sobs into Cornelia's famous lament:

> O noble husband,
> Too great for me to wed, was it my fate
> To bend that lofty head? What prompted me
> To marry you and bring about your fall?
> Now claim your due, and see me gladly pay . . .

So saying she hurried to the altar, quickly took up the veil blessed by the bishop and publicly bound herself to the religious life.

I had still scarcely recovered from my wound when the clerks came thronging round to pester the abbot and myself with repeated demands that I should now for love of God continue the studies which hitherto I had pursued only in desire for wealth and fame. They urged me to consider that the talent entrusted to me by God would be required of me with interest; that instead of addressing myself to the rich as before I should devote myself to educating the poor, and recognize that the hand of the Lord had touched me for the express purpose of freeing me from the temptations of the flesh and the distractions of the world so that I could devote myself to learning, and thereby prove myself a true philosopher not of the world but of God.

But the abbey to which I had withdrawn was completely worldly and depraved, with an abbot whose pre-eminent position was matched by his evil living and notorious reputation. On several occasions I spoke out boldly in criticism of their intolerably foul practices, both in private and in public, and made myself such a burden and nuisance to them all that they gladly seized on the daily importunities of my pupils as a pretext for having me removed from their midst. As pressure continued for some time and these demands became insistent, my abbot and the monks intervened, and I retired to a cell where I could devote myself to teaching as before; and there my pupils gathered in crowds until there were too many for the place to hold or the land to support.

I applied myself mainly to study of the Scriptures as being more suitable to my present calling, but I did not wholly abandon the instruction in the profane arts in which I was better practised and which was most expected of me. In fact I used it as a hook, baited with a taste of philosophy, to draw my listeners towards the study of the true philosophy – the practice of the greatest of Christian philosophers, Origen, as recorded by Eusebius in his *History of the Christian Church*. When it became apparent that God had granted me the gift for interpreting the Scriptures as well as secular literature, the numbers in my school began to increase for both subjects, while elsewhere they diminished rapidly. This roused the envy and hatred of the other heads of schools against me; they set out to disparage me in whatever way they could, and two of them especially were always attacking me behind my back for occupying myself with secular literature in a manner totally unsuitable to my monastic calling, and for presuming to set up as a teacher of sacred learning when I had had no teacher myself. Their aim was for every form of teaching in a school to be forbidden me, and for this end they were always trying to win over bishops, archbishops, abbots, in fact anyone of account in the Church whom they could approach.

Now it happened that I first applied myself to lecturing on the basis of our faith by analogy with human reason, and composed a theological treatise on divine unity and trinity for the use of my students who were asking for human and logical reasons on this subject, and demanded something intelligible rather than mere words. In fact they said that words were useless if the intelligence could not follow them, that nothing could be believed unless it was first understood, and that it was absurd for anyone to preach to others what neither he nor those he taught could grasp with the understanding: the Lord himself had criticized such 'blind guides of blind men'. After the treatise had been seen and read by many people it began to please everyone, as it seemed to answer all questions alike on this subject. It was generally agreed that the questions were peculiarly difficult and the importance of the problem was matched by the subtlety of my solution.

My rivals were therefore much annoyed and convened a Council against me, prompted by my two old opponents, Alberic and Lotulf who, now that our former masters, William and Anselm, were dead, were trying to reign alone in their place and succeed them as their heirs. Both of them were heads of the school in Rheims, and there, by repeated insinuations, they were able to influence their archbishop, Ralph, to take action against me and, along with Conan, bishop of Palestrina, who held the office of papal legate in France at the time, to convene an assembly, which they called a Council, in the city of Soissons, where I was to be invited to come bringing my treatise on the Trinity. This was done, but before I could make my appearance, my two rivals spread such evil rumours about me amongst the clerks and people that I and the few pupils who had accompanied me narrowly escaped being stoned by the people on the first day we arrived, for having preached and written (so they had been told) that there were three Gods.

I called on the legate as soon as I entered the town, handed him a copy of the treatise for him to read and form an opinion, and declared myself ready to receive correction and make amends if I had written anything contrary to the Catholic faith. But he told me at once to take the book to the archbishop and my opponents, so that my accusers could judge me themselves and the words 'Our enemies are judges' be fulfilled in me. However, though they read and reread the book again and again they could find nothing they dared charge me with at an open hearing, so they adjourned the condemnation they were panting for until the final meeting of the Council. For my part, every day before the Council sat, I spoke in public on the Catholic faith in accordance with what I had written, and all who heard me were full of praise both for my exposition and for my interpretation. When the people and clerks saw this they began to say '"Here he is, speaking openly," and no one utters a word against him. The Council which we were told was expressly convened against him is quickly coming to an end. Can the judges have found that the error is theirs, not his?' This went on every day and added fuel to my enemies' fury.

And so one day Alberic sought me out with some of his followers, intent on attacking me. After a few polite words he remarked that something he had noticed in the book had puzzled him very much; namely, that although God begat God, and there is only one God, I denied that God had begotten Himself. I said at once that if they wished I would offer an explanation on this point. 'We take no account of rational explanation,' he answered, 'nor of your interpretation in such matters; we recognize only the words of authority.' 'Turn the page,' I said, 'and you will find the authority.' There was a copy of the book at hand, which he had brought with him, so I looked up the passage which I knew but which he had failed to see – or else he looked only for what would damage me. By God's will I found what I wanted at once: a sentence headed 'Augustine, *On the Trinity*, Book One'. 'Whoever supposes that God has the power to beget Himself is in error, and the more so because it is not only God who lacks this power, but also any spiritual or corporeal creature. There is nothing whatsoever which can beget itself.'

When his followers standing by heard this they blushed in embarrassment, but he tried to cover up his mistake as best he could by saying that this should be understood in the right way. To that I replied that it was nothing new, but was irrelevant at the moment as he was looking only for words, not interpretation. But if he was willing to hear an interpretation and a reasoned argument I was ready to prove to him that by his own words he had fallen into the heresy of supposing the Father to be His own Son. On hearing this he lost his temper and turned to threats, crying that neither my explanations nor my authorities would help me in this case. He then went off.

On the last day of the Council, before the session was resumed, the legate and the archbishop began to discuss at length with my opponents and other persons what decision to take about me and my book, as this was the chief reason for their being convened. They could find nothing to bring against me either in my words or in the treatise which was before them, and everyone stood silent for a while or began to retract his accusation, until Geoffrey, bishop of Chartres, who was outstanding among the other bishops for his reputation for holiness and the importance of his see, spoke as follows:

All of you, Sirs, who are here today know that this man's teaching, whatever it is, and his intellectual ability have won him many followers and supporters wherever he has studied. He has greatly lessened the reputation both of his own teachers and of ours, and his vine has spread its branches from sea to sea. If you injure him through prejudice, though I do not think you will, you must know that even if your judgement is deserved you will offend many people, and large numbers will rally to his defence; especially as in this treatise before us we can see nothing which deserves any public condemnation. Jerome has said that 'Courage which is unconcealed always attracts envy, and lightning strikes the mountain-peaks.' Beware lest violent action on your part brings him even more renown, and we are more damaged ourselves for our envy than he is through the justice of the charge. Jerome also reminds us that 'A false rumour is soon stifled, and a man's later life passes judgement on his past.' But if you are determined to act canonically against him, let his teaching or his writing be put before us, let him be questioned and allowed to give free reply, so that if he is convicted or confesses his error he can be totally silenced. This will at least be in accordance with the words of holy Nicodemus, when he wished to set free the Lord himself: 'Does our law permit us to pass judgement on a man unless we have first given him a hearing and learned the facts?'

At once my rivals broke in with an outcry: 'Fine advice that is, to bid us compete with the ready tongue of a man whose arguments and sophistries could triumph over the whole world!' (But it was surely far harder to compete with Christ, and yet Nicodemus asked for him to be given a hearing, as sanctioned by the law.) However, when the bishop could not persuade them to agree to his proposal, he tried to curb their hostility by other means, saying that the few people present were insufficient for discussing a matter of such importance, and this case needed longer consideration. His further advice was that my abbot, who was present, should take me back to my monastery, the Abbey of St Denis, and there a larger number of more learned men should be assembled to go into the case thoroughly and decide what was to be done. The legate agreed with this last suggestion, and so did everyone else. Soon after, the legate rose to celebrate Mass before he opened the Council. Through Bishop Geoffrey he sent me the permission agreed on: I was to return to my monastery and await a decision.

Then my rivals, thinking that they had achieved nothing if this matter were taken outside their diocese, where they would have no power to use force – it was plain that they had little confidence in the justice of their cause – convinced the archbishop that it would be an insult to his dignity if the case were transferred and heard elsewhere, and a serious danger if I were allowed to escape as a result. They hurried to the legate, made him reverse his decision and persuaded him against his better judgement to condemn the book without any inquiry, burn it immediately in the sight of all and condemn me to perpetual confinement in a different monastery. They said that the fact that I had dared to read the treatise in public and must have allowed many people to make copies without its being approved by the authority of the Pope or the Church should be quite enough to condemn it, and that the Christian faith would greatly benefit if an example were made of me and similar presumption in many others were forestalled. As the legate was less of a scholar than he should have been, he relied largely on the advice of the archbishop, who in turn relied on theirs. When the bishop of Chartres saw what would happen he told me at once about their intrigues and strongly urged me not to take it too hard, as by now it was apparent to all that they were acting too harshly. He said I could be confident that such violence so clearly prompted by jealousy would discredit them and benefit me, and told me not to worry about being confined in a monastery as he knew that the papal legate was only acting under pressure, and would set me quite free within a few days of his leaving Soissons. So he gave me what comfort he could, both of us shedding tears.

I was then summoned and came at once before the Council. Without any questioning or discussion they compelled me to throw my book into the fire with my own hands, and so it was burnt. But so that they could appear to have something to say, one of my enemies muttered that he understood it was written in the book that only God the Father was Almighty. Overhearing this, the legate replied in great surprise that one would scarcely believe a small child could make such a mistake, seeing that it is a professed tenet of our common faith that there are three Almighties. Thereupon the head of a school, Thierry by name, laughed and quoted the words of Athanasius: 'And yet there are not three Almighties, but one Almighty.' His bishop spoke sharply to him and rebuked him for contempt of court, but he boldly stood his ground and, in the words of Daniel: '"Are you such fools, you Israelites, thus to condemn a woman of Israel, without making careful

inquiry and finding out the truth? Reopen the trial,"'
he said, 'and judge the judge himself. You appointed
this judge for the establishment of the Faith and the
correction of error; but the person who should be doing
the judging has condemned himself out of his own
mouth. Today God in his mercy clearly acquits this
innocent man as he delivered Susanna of old from the
hands of her false accusers!'

Then the archbishop rose to his feet and confirmed
the opinion of the legate, changing only the wording,
as was needed. 'Truly, my lord,' he said, 'the Father is
Almighty, the Son is Almighty and the Holy Spirit
is Almighty, and whoever does not share this belief is
clearly in error and should not be heard. And now, with
your permission, it would be proper for our brother to
profess his faith before us all, so that it may be duly
approved or disapproved and corrected.' I then stood
up to make a full profession of my faith and explain
what I felt in my own words, but my enemies declared
that it was only necessary for me to recite the Atha-
nasian Creed – as any boy could do. They even had
the text put before me to read in case I should plead
ignorance, as though I were not familiar with the
words. I read it out as best I could through my tears,
choked with sobs. Then I was handed over as if guilty
and condemned to the abbot of St Médard, who was
present, and taken off to his cloister as if to prison.
The Council then immediately dispersed.

The abbot and monks of St Médard welcomed me
most warmly and treated me with every consideration,
thinking that I should remain with them in future.

They tried hard to comfort me, but in vain. God who judges equity, with what bitterness of spirit and anguish of mind did I reproach you in my madness and accuse you in my fury, constantly repeating the lament of St Antony – 'Good Jesus, where were you?' All the grief and indignation, the blushes for shame, the agony of despair I suffered then I cannot put into words. I compared my present plight with my physical suffering in the past, and judged myself the unhappiest of men. My former betrayal seemed small in comparison with the wrongs I now had to endure, and I wept much more for the injury done to my reputation than for the damage to my body, for that I had brought upon myself through my own fault, but this open violence had come upon me only because of the purity of my intentions and love of our Faith which had compelled me to write.

But as the news spread and everyone who heard it began to condemn outright this wanton act of cruelty, the persons who had been present tried to shift the blame on to others; so much so that even my rivals denied it had been done on their advice, and the legate publicly denounced the jealousy of the French in this affair. He soon regretted his conduct and, some days later, feeling that he had satisfied their jealousy at a time when under constraint, he had me brought out of St Médard and sent back to my own monastery, where, as I said above, nearly all the monks who were there before were now my enemies; for their disgraceful way of life and scandalous practices made them deeply suspicious of a man whose criticisms they could ill endure.

A few months later chance gave them the opportunity to work for my downfall. It happened that one day in my reading I came across a statement of Bede, in his *Commentary on the Acts of the Apostles*, which asserted that Dionysius the Areopagite was bishop of Corinth, not of Athens. This seemed in direct contradiction to their claim that their patron Denis is to be identified with the famous Areopagite whose history shows him to have been bishop of Athens. I showed my discovery, by way of a joke, to some of the brothers who were standing by, as evidence from Bede which was against us. They were very much annoyed and said that Bede was a complete liar and they had a more truthful witness in their own abbot Hilduin, who had spent a long time travelling in Greece to investigate the matter; he had found out the truth and removed all shadow of doubt in the history of the saint which he had compiled himself. Then one of them abruptly demanded my opinion on the discrepancy between Bede and Hilduin. I replied that the authority of Bede, whose writings are accepted by the entire Latin Church, carried more weight with me.

In their fury at this answer they began to cry that now I had openly revealed myself as the enemy of the monastery, and was moreover a traitor to the whole country in seeking to destroy the glory that was its special pride by denying that their patron was the Areopagite. I said that I had not denied it, nor did it much matter whether he was the Areopagite or came from somewhere else, seeing that he had won so bright a crown in the eyes of God. However, they hurried straight to the abbot and told him what they accused me of. He was only too ready to listen and delighted to seize the opportunity to destroy me, for he had the greater reason to fear me as his own life was even more scandalous than that of the rest. He summoned his council, and the chapter of the brethren, and denounced me severely, saying that he would send me straightaway to the king for punishment on the charge of having designs on the royal dignity and crown. Meanwhile he put me under close surveillance until I could be handed over to the king. I offered to submit myself to the discipline of the Rule if I had done wrong, but in vain.

I was so horrified by their wickedness and in such deep despair after having borne the blows of fortune so long, feeling that the whole world had conspired against me, that with the help of a few brothers who took pity on me and the support of some of my pupils I fled secretly in the night, and took refuge in the neighbouring territory of Count Theobald, where once before I had stayed in a priory. I was slightly acquainted with the Count personally, and he had heard of my afflictions and took pity on me. There I began to live in the town of Provins, in a community of monks from Troyes whose prior had long been my close friend and loved me dearly. He was overjoyed by my arrival and made every provision for me.

But one day it happened that the abbot of St Denis came to the town to see Count Theobald on some personal business; on hearing this, I approached the count, along with the prior, and begged him to intercede for me with the abbot and obtain his pardon and permission to live a monastic life wherever a suitable place could be found. The abbot and those with him took counsel together on the matter, so as to give the count their answer the same day, before they left. On deliberation they formed the opinion that my intention was to be transferred to another abbey and that this would be a great reproach to them, for they considered that I had brought them great glory when I entered the religious life by coming to them in preference to all other abbeys, and now it would be a serious disgrace if I cast them off and went elsewhere. Consequently they would not hear a word on the subject either from the count or from me. Moreover they threatened me with excommunication if I did not return quickly, and absolutely forbade the prior with whom I had taken refuge to keep me any longer, under penalty of sharing my excommunication.

Both the prior and I were very much alarmed at this. The abbot departed, still in the same mind, and a few days later he died. When his successor was appointed, I met him with the bishop of Meaux, hoping that he would grant what I had sought from his predecessor. He too was unwilling to do so at first; but through the intervention of some of my friends I appealed to the king and his council, and so got what I wanted. A certain Stephen, the king's seneschal at the time, summoned the abbot and his supporters and asked why they wished to hold me against my will when this could easily involve them in scandal and do no good, as my life and theirs could never possibly agree. I knew that the opinion of the king's council was that the more irregular an abbey was, the more reason why it should be subject to the king and bring him profit, at least as regards its worldly goods, and this made me think that I should easily win the consent of the king and his council – which I did. But so that the monastery should not lose the reputation gained from having me as a member, I was given permission to withdraw to any retreat I liked, provided that I did not come under the authority of any abbey. This was agreed and confirmed on both sides in the presence of the king and his council.

And so I took myself off to a lonely spot I had known before in the territory of Troyes, and there, on a piece of land given me, by leave of the local bishop, I built a sort of oratory of reeds and thatch and dedicated it in the name of the Holy Trinity. Here I could stay hidden alone but for one of my clerks, and truly cry out to the Lord 'Lo, I escaped far away and found a refuge in the wilderness.'

No sooner was this known than the students began to gather there from all parts, hurrying from cities and towns to inhabit the wilderness, leaving large mansions to build themselves little huts, eating wild herbs and coarse bread instead of delicate food, spreading reeds and straw in place of soft beds and using banks of turf for tables. They could rightly be thought of as imitating the early philosophers, of whom Jerome in the second book of his *Against Jovinian* says:

The senses are like windows through which the vices gain entry into the soul. The capital and citadel of the spirit cannot be taken except by a hostile army entering through the gates. If anyone takes pleasure in the circus and athletic contests, an actor's pantomime or a woman's beauty, the splendour of jewels and garments or anything of that sort, the liberty of his soul is captured through the window of the eye, and the word of the prophet is fulfilled: 'Death has climbed in through our windows.' So when the marshalled forces of distraction have marched through these gates into the citadel of the soul, where will its liberty be and its fortitude? Where will be its thoughts of God? Especially when sensibility pictures for itself pleasures of the past and by recalling its vices compels the soul to take part in them and, as it were, to practise what it does not actually do. These are the considerations which have led many philosophers to leave crowded cities and the gardens outside them, where they find that water meadows and leafy trees, twittering of birds, reflections in spring waters and murmuring brooks are so many snares for eye and ear; they fear that amidst all this abundance of riches the strength of the soul will weaken and its purity be soiled. No good comes from looking often on what may one day seduce you, and in exposing yourself to the temptation of what you find it difficult to do without. Indeed, the Pythagoreans used to shun this kind of contact and lived in solitude in the desert. Plato himself was a wealthy man (and his couch was trampled on by Diogenes with muddy feet), yet in order to give all his time to philosophy he chose to set up his Academy some way from the city on a site which was unhealthy as well as deserted, so that the perpetual preoccupation of sickness would break the assaults of lust, and his pupils would know no pleasures but what they had from their studies.

*

Such too was the life that the sons of the prophets, the followers of Elisha, are said to have led, of whom (amongst other things) Jerome writes to the monk Rusticus, as if they were the monks of their time, that 'The sons of the prophets, who are called monks in the Old Testament, built themselves huts by the river Jordan, and abandoned city crowds to live on barley meal and wild herbs.' My pupils built themselves similar huts on the banks of the Ardusson, and looked like hermits rather than scholars.

But the greater the crowds of students who gathered there and the harder the life they led under my teaching, the more my rivals thought this brought honour to me and shame upon themselves. They had done all they could to harm me, and now they could not bear to see things turning out for my advantage; and so, in the words of Jerome: 'Remote as I was from cities, public affairs, law-courts and crowds, envy (as Quintilian says) sought me out in my retreat.' They brooded silently over their wrongs, and then began to complain '"Why, all the world has gone after him" – we have gained nothing by persecuting him, only increased his fame. We meant to extinguish the light of his name but all we have done is make it shine still brighter. See how the students have everything they need at hand in the cities, but they scorn the comforts of civilization, flock to the barren wilderness and choose this wretched life of their own accord.'

Now it was sheer pressure of poverty at the time which determined me to open a school, since I was 'not strong enough to dig and too proud to beg'; so I returned to the skill which I knew, and made use of my tongue instead of working with my hands. For their part, my pupils provided all I needed unasked, food, clothing, work on the land as well as building expenses, so that I should not be kept from my studies by domestic cares of any kind. As my oratory could not hold even a modest proportion of their numbers, they were obliged to enlarge it, and improved it by building in wood and stone. It had been founded and dedicated in the name of the Holy Trinity, but because I had come there as a fugitive and in the depths of my despair had been granted some comfort by the grace of God, I named it the Paraclete, in memory of this gift. Many who heard the name were astonished, and several people violently attacked me, on the grounds that it was not permissible for my church to be assigned specifically to the Holy Spirit any more than to God the Father, but that it must be dedicated according to ancient custom either to the Son alone or to the whole Trinity.

This false charge doubtless arose from their mistaken belief that there was no distinction between the Paraclete and the Holy Spirit as Paraclete. In fact, the whole Trinity or any member of the Trinity may be addressed as God and Protector and equally properly be addressed as Paraclete, that is, Comforter, according to the words of the Apostle: 'Praise be to the God and Father of our Lord Jesus Christ, the all-merciful Father and the God whose consolation never fails us. He comforts us in all our troubles; and as the Truth says, "And he shall give you another to be your Comforter."' When the whole Church is consecrated in the name of the Father and of the Son and of the Holy Spirit, and is in their possession indivisibly, what is to prevent the house of the Lord from being ascribed to the Father or to the Holy Spirit just as much as to the Son? Who would presume to erase the owner's name from above his door? Or again, when the Son has offered himself as a sacrifice to the Father, and consequently, in celebrations of the Mass it is the Father to whom prayers are specially directed and the Host is offered, why should the altar not properly be particularly his to whom prayer and sacrifice are specially offered? Is it any better to say that the altar belongs to him who is sacrificed than to him to whom sacrifice is made? Would anyone claim that an altar is better named after the Lord's Cross, or the Sepulchre, St Michael, St John or St Peter, or any other saint who is neither sacrificed there nor receives sacrifice, nor has prayers addressed to him? Surely even amongst the idolators, altars and temples were said to belong only to those who received sacrifice and homage. Perhaps someone may say that neither churches nor altars should be dedicated to the Father because no deed of his exists which calls for a special feast in his honour. But this argument detracts from the entire Trinity, not from the Holy Spirit, since the Holy Spirit by its coming has its own feast of Pentecost, just as the Son, by his, has the feast of the Nativity; for the Holy Spirit claims its own feast by coming among the disciples just as the Son came into the world.

In fact it seems more fitting that a temple should be ascribed to the Holy Spirit than to any other member of the Trinity, if we pay careful attention to apostolic authority and the workings of the Holy Spirit itself. To none of the three does the Apostle assign a special shrine except to the Holy Spirit, for he speaks neither of a shrine of the Father nor of the Son as he does of the Holy Spirit when he writes in the First Letter to the Corinthians: 'But he who links himself with Christ is one with him, spiritually,' and again, 'Do you not know that your body is a shrine of the in-dwelling Holy Spirit, and the spirit is God's gift to you? You do not belong to yourselves.' Everyone knows too that the divine benefits of the sacraments administered in the Church are ascribed particularly to the effective power of divine Grace, by which is meant the Holy Spirit. For by water and the Holy Spirit we are reborn in baptism, after which we first become a special temple for God; and in the sacrament of confirmation the sevenfold grace of the Holy Spirit is conferred on us whereby the temple of God is adorned and dedicated. Is it then surprising that we dedicate a material temple to the one to whom the Apostle has specially ascribed a spiritual one? To whom can a church be more fittingly consecrated than to the one to whose effective power all the benefits of the Church sacraments are particularly ascribed? However, in first giving my oratory the name of Paraclete I had no thought of declaring its dedication to a single person; my reason was simply what I said above – it was in memory of the comfort I had found there. But even if I had done so with the intention that was generally believed, it would not have been unreasonable, though unknown to general custom.

Meanwhile, though my person lay hidden in this place, my fame travelled all over the world, resounding everywhere like that poetic creation Echo, so called because she has so large a voice but no substance. My former rivals could do nothing by themselves, and therefore stirred up against me some new apostles in whom the world had great faith. One of these boasted that he had reformed the life of the Canons Regular, the other the life of the monks. They went up and down the country, slandering me shamelessly in their preaching as much as they could, and for a while brought me into considerable disrepute in the eyes of the ecclesiastical as well as of the secular authorities; and they spread such evil reports of my faith and of my way of life that they also turned some of my chief friends against me, while any who up till now had retained some of their old affection for me took fright and tried to conceal this as best they could. God is my witness that I never heard that an assembly of ecclesiastics had met without thinking this was convened to condemn me. I waited like one in terror of being struck by lightning to be brought before a council or synod and charged with heresy or profanity, and, if I may compare the flea with the lion, the ant with the elephant, my rivals persecuted me with the same cruelty as the heretics in the past did St Athanasius. Often, God knows, I fell into such a state of despair that I thought of quitting the realm of Christendom and going over to the heathen, there to live a quiet Christian life amongst the enemies of Christ at the cost of what tribute was asked. I told myself they would receive me more kindly for having no suspicion that I was a Christian on account of the charges against me, and they would therefore believe I could more easily be won over to their pagan beliefs.

While I was continuously harassed by these anxieties and as a last resort had thought of taking refuge with Christ among Christ's enemies, an opportunity was offered me which I believed would bring me some respite from the plots against me; but in taking it I fell among Christians and monks who were far more savage and wicked than the heathen. There was in Brittany, in the diocese of Vannes, the Abbey of St Gildas de Rhuys, which the death of its abbot had left without a superior. I was invited there by the unanimous choice of the monks, with the approval of the lord of the district, and permission from the abbot and brothers of my monastery was easily obtained. Thus the jealousy of the French drove me West as that of the Romans once drove St Jerome East. God knows, I should never have accepted this offer had I not hoped to find some escape from the attacks which, as I said, I had perpetually to endure. The country was wild and the language unknown to me, the natives were brutal and barbarous, the monks were beyond control and led a dissolute life which was well known to all. Like a man who rushes at a precipice in terror at the sword hanging over him, and at the very moment he escapes one death, meets another, I wilfully took myself from one danger to another, and there by the fearful roar of the waves of the Ocean, at the far ends of the earth where I could flee no further, I used to repeat in my prayers the words of the Psalmist: 'From the end of the earth I have called to thee when my heart was in anguish.'

Everyone knows now, I think, of this anguish which my tormented heart suffered night and day at the hands of that undisciplined community I had undertaken to direct, while I thought of the dangers to my soul as well as to my body. I was certain at any rate that if I tried to bring them back to the life of Rule for which they had taken their vows it would cost me my own life; yet if I did not do my utmost to achieve this, I should be damned. In addition, the abbey had long been subject to a certain very powerful tyrant in that land who had taken advantage of the disorder in the monastery to appropriate all its adjoining lands for his own use, and was exacting heavier taxes from the monks than he would have done from Jews subject to tribute. The monks beset me with demands for their daily needs, though there was no common allowance for me to distribute, but each one of them provided for himself, his concubine and his sons and daughters from his own purse. They took delight in distressing me over this, and they also stole and carried off what they could, so that when I had reached the end of my resources I should be forced to abandon my attempt at enforcing discipline or leave them altogether. The entire savage population of the area was similarly lawless and out of control; there was no one I could turn to for help since I disapproved equally of the morals of them all. Outside the monastery wall that tyrant and his minions never ceased to harry me, inside it the monks were always setting traps for me, until it seemed

45

that the words of the Apostle applied especially to my case: 'Quarrels all round us, forebodings in our heart.'

I used to weep as I thought of the wretched, useless life I led, as profitless to myself as to others; I had once done so much for the clerks, and now that I had abandoned them for the monastery, all I did for them and for the monks was equally fruitless. I had proved ineffective in all my attempts and undertakings, so that now above all men I justly merited the reproach, 'There is the man who started to build and could not finish.' I was in deep despair when I remembered what I had fled from and considered what I had met with now; my former troubles were as nothing in retrospect, and I often used to groan and tell myself that I deserved my present sufferings for deserting the Paraclete, the Comforter, and plunging myself into certain desolation – in my eagerness to escape from threats I had run into actual dangers.

What tormented me most of all was the thought that in abandoning my oratory I had been unable to make proper provision for celebrating the Divine Office, since the place was so poor that it could barely provide for the needs of one man. But then again the true Paraclete himself brought me true comfort in my great distress, and provided for the oratory as was fitting, for it was his own. It happened that my abbot of St Denis by some means took possession of the Abbey of Argenteuil where Heloise – now my sister in Christ rather than my wife – had taken the veil. He claimed that it belonged to his monastery by ancient right, and forcibly expelled the community of nuns, of which she was prioress, so that they were now scattered as exiles in various places. I realized that this was an opportunity sent me by the Lord for providing for my oratory, and so I returned and invited her, along with some other nuns from the same convent who would not leave her, to come to the Paraclete; and once they had gathered there, I handed it over to them as a gift, and also everything that went with it. Subsequently, with the approval of the local bishop acting as intermediary, my deed of gift was confirmed by Pope Innocent the Second by charter in perpetuity to them and their successors.

Their life there was full of hardship at first and for a while they suffered the greatest deprivation, but soon God, whom they served devoutly, in his mercy brought them comfort; he showed himself a true Paraclete to them too in making the local people sympathetic and kindly disposed towards them. Indeed, I fancy that their worldly goods were multiplied more in a single year than mine would have been in a hundred, had I remained there, for a woman, being the weaker sex, is the more pitiable in a state of need, easily rousing human sympathy, and her virtue is the more pleasing to God as it is to man. And such favour in the eyes of all did God bestow on that sister of mine who was in charge of the other nuns, that bishops loved her as a daughter, abbots as a sister, the laity as a mother; while all alike admired her piety and wisdom, and her unequalled gentleness and patience in every situation. The more rarely she allowed herself to be seen (so that she could devote herself without distraction to prayer and meditation on holy things in a closed cell), the more eagerly did those outside demand her presence and her spiritual conversation for their guidance.

But then all the people in the neighbourhood began attacking me violently for doing less than I could and should to minister to the needs of the women, as (they said) I was certainly well able to do, if only through my preaching; so I started to visit them more often to see how I could help them. This provoked malicious insinuations, and my detractors, with their usual perverseness, had the effrontery to accuse me of doing what genuine charity prompted because I was still a slave to the pleasures of carnal desire and could rarely or never bear the absence of the woman I had once loved. I often repeated to myself the lament of St Jerome in his letter to Asella about false friends: 'The only fault found in me is my sex, and that only when Paula comes to Jerusalem.' And again: 'Before I knew the house of saintly Paula, my praises were sung throughout the city, and nearly everyone judged me worthy of the highest office of the Church. But I know well that it is through good and evil report that we make our way to the kingdom of heaven.'

When, as I say, I recalled the injustice of such a calumny against so great a man, I took no small comfort from it. 'If my rivals,' said I, 'were to find such strong grounds for suspicion in my case, how I should suffer from their slander! But now that I have been freed from such suspicion by God's mercy, and the power to commit this sin is taken from me, how can the suspicion remain? What is the meaning of this latest monstrous accusation? My present condition removes suspicion of evil-doing so completely from everyone's mind that men who wish to keep close watch on their wives employ eunuchs, as sacred history tells us in the case of Esther and the other concubines of King Ahasuerus. We also read that it was a eunuch of the Ethiopian Queen Candace, a man of authority in charge of all her treasure, whom the apostle Philip was directed by the angel to convert and baptize. Such men have always held positions of responsibility and familiarity in the homes of modest and honourable women simply because they are far removed from suspicions of this kind, and it was to rid himself of it entirely, when planning to include women in his teaching of sacred learning, that the great Christian philosopher Origen laid violent hands on himself, as Book Six of the *History of the Church* relates.' However, I thought that in this God's mercy had been kinder to me than to him, for he is believed to have acted on impulse and been strongly censured as a result, whereas it had happened to me through no fault of mine, but so that I might be set free for a similar work; and with all the less pain for being quick and sudden, for I was asleep when attacked and felt practically nothing.

Yet though perhaps I suffered less physical pain at the time, I am now the more distressed for the calumny I must endure. My agony is less for the mutilation of my body than for the damage to my reputation, for it is written that 'A good name is more to be desired than great riches.' In his sermon *On the Life and Morals of Clerics* St Augustine remarks that 'He who relies on his conscience to the neglect of his reputation is cruel to himself,' and earlier on says: '"For our aims," as the Apostle says, "are honourable not only in God's sight but also in the eyes of men." For ourselves, our conscience within us is sufficient. For your sake, our reputation should not be sullied but should be powerful amongst you. Conscience and reputation are two different things; conscience concerns yourself, reputation your neighbour.' But what would my enemies in their malice have said to Christ himself and his followers, to the prophets, the apostles or the other holy Fathers, had they lived in their times, when these men were seen with their manhood intact consorting with women on the friendliest terms? Here also St Augustine in his book *On the Work of Monks* proves that women too were the inseparable companions of our Lord Jesus Christ and the apostles, even to the extent of accompanying them on their preaching:

To this end, faithful women who had worldly goods went with them and made provision for them so that they should lack none of the necessities of this life. If anyone does not believe that it was the practice of the apostles to take with them women of holy life wherever they preached the Gospel, he has only to hear the Gospel to know that they did this following the example of the Lord himself. For there it is written: 'After this he went journeying from town to town and village to village, proclaiming the good news of God. With him were the Twelve and a number of women who had been set free from evil spirits and infirmities: Mary, known as Mary of Magdala . . . Joanna, the wife of Chuza,

Herod's steward, and Susanna, and many others. These women provided for them out of their own resources.'

Leo the Ninth too, in answer to a letter of Parmenian, of the monastery of Studius, says:

We declare absolutely that no bishop, presbyter, deacon or subdeacon may give up the care of his wife in the name of religion, so as not to provide her with food and clothing, though he may not lie with her carnally. This was the practice of the holy apostles, as we read in St Paul: 'Have I no right to take a Christian wife about with me, like the rest of the apostles and the Lord's brothers and Cephas?' Take note, you fool, that he did not say 'Have I no right to embrace a wife' but 'to take about', meaning that they should support their wives on the profit from their preaching, not that they should have further carnal intercourse with them.

Certainly that Pharisee who said to himself of the Lord, 'If this man were a real prophet he would know who this woman is who touches him, and what sort of woman she is, a sinner,' could have supposed far more easily, as far as human judgement goes, that the Lord was guilty of evil-living than my enemies could imagine the same of me; while anyone who saw the Lord's mother entrusted to the care of a young man or the prophets enjoying the hospitality and conversation of widows would entertain far more probable suspicions. And what would my detractors have said if they had seen Malchus, the captive monk of whom St Jerome writes, living in the same home with his wife? In their eyes it would have been a great crime, though the famous doctor had nothing but high praise for what he saw: 'There was an old man named Malchus there . . . a native of the place, and an old woman living in his cottage . . . Both of them were so eager for the faith, for ever wearing down the threshold of the church, that you would have thought them Zacharias and Elizabeth in the Gospel but for the fact that John was not with them.'

Finally, why do they refrain from accusing the holy Fathers themselves, when we have often read or seen how they founded monasteries for women too and ministered to them there, following the example of the seven deacons, who were appointed to wait at table and look after the women? The weaker sex needs the help of the stronger, so much so that the Apostle lays down that the man must always be over the woman, as her head, and as a sign of this he orders her always to have her head covered. And so I am much surprised that the custom should have been long established in convents of putting abbesses in charge of women just as abbots are set over men, and of binding women by profession according to the same rule, for there is so much in the Rule which cannot be carried out by women, whether in authority or subordinate. In several places too, the natural order is overthrown to the extent that we see abbesses and nuns ruling the clergy who have authority over the people, with opportunities of leading them on to evil desires in proportion to their dominance, holding them as they do beneath a heavy yoke. The satirist has this in mind when he says that 'Nothing is more intolerable than a rich woman.'

After much reflection I decided to do all I could to provide for the sisters of the Paraclete, to manage their affairs, to watch over them in person too, so that they would revere me the more, and thus to minister better to their needs. The persecution I was now suffering at the hands of the monks who were my sons was even more persistent and distressing than what I had endured previously from my brothers, so I thought I could turn to the sisters as a haven of peace and safety from the raging storms, find repose there for a while, and at least achieve something amongst them though I had failed with the monks. Indeed, the more they needed me in their weakness, the more it would benefit me.

But now Satan has put so many obstacles in my path that I can find nowhere to rest or even to live; a fugitive and wanderer I carry everywhere the curse of Cain, forever tormented (as I said above) by 'quarrels all round us, forebodings in our heart', or rather, quarrels and forebodings without and within. The hostility of my sons here is far more relentless and dangerous than that of my enemies, for I have them always with me and must be forever on my guard against their treachery. I can see my enemies' violence as a danger to my person if I go outside the cloister; but it is within the cloister that I have to face the incessant assaults – as crafty as they are violent – of my sons, that is, of the monks entrusted to my care, as their abbot and father. How many times have they tried to poison me – as happened to St Benedict! The same reason which led him to abandon his depraved sons might well have encouraged me to follow the example of so great a Father of the Church, lest in exposing myself to certain dangers I should be thought a rash tempter rather than a true lover of God, or even appear to be my own destroyer. And while I guarded as well as I could against their daily assaults by providing my own food and drink, they tried to destroy me during the very sacrifice of the altar by putting poison in the chalice. On another day, when I had gone into Nantes to visit the count who was ill, and was staying there in the home of one of my brothers in the flesh, they tried to poison me by the hand of one of the servants accompanying me, supposing, no doubt, that I should be less on my guard against a plot of that kind. By God's intervention it happened that I did not touch any of the food prepared for me. But one of the monks I had brought from the abbey, who knew nothing of their intentions, ate it and dropped dead; and the servant who had dared to do this fled in terror, as much through consciousness of his guilt as because of the evidence of his crime.

From then on their villainy was known to all, and I began to make no secret of the fact that I was avoiding their snares as well as I could; I even removed myself from the abbey and lived in small cells with a few companions. But whenever the monks heard that I was travelling anywhere they would bribe robbers and station them on the roads and byways to murder me. I was still struggling against all these perils when one day the hand of the Lord struck me sharply and I fell from my saddle, breaking my collar-bone. This fracture caused me far greater pain and weakened me more than my previous injury. Sometimes I tried to put a stop to their lawless insubordination by excommunication, and compelled those of them I most feared to promise me either on their honour or on oath taken before the rest that they would leave the abbey altogether and trouble me no more. But then they would openly and shamelessly violate both the word they had given and the oaths they had sworn, until in the end they were forced to renew their oaths on this and many other things in the presence of the count and the bishops, by authority of the Roman Pope Innocent, through his special legate sent for this purpose.

Even then they would not live in peace. After those mentioned had been expelled, I recently came back to the abbey and entrusted myself to the remaining brothers from whom I thought I had less to fear. I found them even worse than the others. They did not deal with poison but with a dagger held to my throat, and it was only under the protection of a certain lord of the land that I managed to escape. I am still in danger, and every day I imagine a sword hanging over my head, so that at meals I dare scarcely breathe: like the man we read about, who supposed the power and wealth of the tyrant Dionysius to constitute the greatest happiness, until he looked up and saw a sword suspended by a thread over Dionysius's head. Then he learned what sort of joy it is which accompanies earthly power. This is my experience all the time; a poor monk raised to be an abbot, the more wretched as I have become more wealthy, in order that my example may curb the ambition of those who have deliberately chosen a similar course.

Dearly beloved brother in Christ, close friend and long-standing companion, this is the story of my misfortunes which have dogged me almost since I left my cradle; let the fact that I have written it with your own affliction and the injury you have suffered in mind suffice to enable you (as I said at the beginning of this letter) to think of your trouble as little or nothing in comparison with mine, and to bear it with more patience when you can see it in proportion. Take comfort from what the Lord told his followers about the followers of the Devil: 'As they persecuted me they will persecute you. If the world hates you, it hated me first, as you know well. If you belonged to the world, the world would love its own.' And the Apostle says: 'Persecution will come to all who want to live a godly life as Christians,' and elsewhere, 'Do you think I am currying favour with men? If I still sought men's favour I should be no servant of Christ.' The Psalmist says that 'They are destroyed who seek to please men, since God has rejected them.' It was with this particularly in mind that St Jerome, whose heir I consider myself as regards slanders and false accusations, wrote in his letter to Nepotian: '"If I still sought men's favour," says the Apostle, "I should be no servant of Christ." He has ceased to seek men's favour and is become the servant of Christ.' He also wrote to Asella, concerning false friends, 'Thank God I have deserved the hatred of the world,' and to the monk Heliodorus: 'You are wrong, brother, wrong if you think that the Christian can ever be free of persecution. Our adversary "like a roaring lion, prowls around, seeking someone to devour", and do you think of peace? "He sits in ambush with the rich."'

Let us then take heart from these proofs and examples, and bear our wrongs the more cheerfully the more we know they are undeserved. Let us not doubt that if they add nothing to our merit, at least they contribute to the expiation of our sins. And since everything is managed by divine ordinance, each one of the faithful, when it comes to the test, must take comfort at least from the knowledge that God's supreme goodness allows nothing to be done outside his plan, and whatever is started wrongly, he himself brings it to the best conclusion. Hence in all things it is right to say to him, 'Thy will be done.' Finally, think what consolation comes to those who love God on the authority of the Apostle, who says: 'As we know, all things work together for good for those who love God.' This is what the wisest of mankind had in mind when he said in his *Proverbs*: 'Whatever befalls the righteous man it shall not sadden him.' Here he clearly shows that those who are angered by some personal injury, though they well know it has been laid on them by divine dispensation, leave the path of righteousness and follow their own will rather than God's; they rebel in their secret hearts against the meaning of the words 'Thy will be done', and set their own will above the will of God. Farewell.

LETTER 2

Heloise to Abelard: Fresh Wounds of Grief

Not long ago, my beloved, by chance someone brought me the letter of consolation you had sent to a friend. I saw at once from the superscription that it was yours, and was all the more eager to read it since the writer is so dear to my heart. I hoped for renewal of strength, at least from the writer's words which would picture for me the reality I have lost. But nearly every line of this letter was filled, I remember, with gall and wormwood, as it told the pitiful story of our entry into religion and the cross of unending suffering which you, my only love, continue to bear.

In that letter you did indeed carry out the promise you made your friend at the beginning, that he would think his own troubles insignificant or nothing, in comparison with your own. First you revealed the persecution you suffered from your teachers, then the supreme treachery of the mutilation of your person, and then described the abominable jealousy and violent attacks of your fellow-students, Alberic of Rheims and Lotulf of Lombardy. You did not gloss over what at their instigation was done to your distinguished theological work or what amounted to a prison sentence passed on yourself. Then you went on to the plotting against you by your abbot and false brethren, the serious slanders from those two pseudo-apostles, spread against you by the same rivals, and the scandal stirred up among many people because you had acted contrary to custom in naming your oratory after the Paraclete. You went on to the incessant, intolerable persecutions which you still endure at the hands of that cruel tyrant and the evil monks you call your sons, and so brought your sad story to an end.

No one, I think, could read or hear it dry-eyed; my own sorrows are renewed by the detail in which you have told it, and redoubled because you say your perils are still increasing. All of us here are driven to despair of your life, and every day we await in fear and trembling the final word of your death. And so in the name of Christ, who is still giving you some protection for his service, we beseech you to write as often as you think fit to us who are his handmaids and yours, with news of the perils in which you are still storm-tossed. We are all that are left you, so at least you should let us share your sorrow or your joy.

It is always some consolation in sorrow to feel that it is shared, and any burden laid on several is carried more lightly or removed. And if this storm has quietened down for a while, you must be all the more prompt to send us a letter which will be the more gladly received. But whatever you write about will bring us no small relief in the mere proof that you have us in mind. Letters from absent friends are welcome indeed, as Seneca himself shows us by his own example when he writes these words in a passage of a letter to his friend Lucilius:

Thank you for writing to me often, the one way in which you can make your presence felt, for I never have a letter from you without the immediate feeling that we are together. If pictures of absent friends give us pleasure, renewing our memories and relieving the pain of separation even if they cheat us with empty comfort, how much more welcome is a letter which comes to us in the very handwriting of an absent friend.

Thank God that here at least is a way of restoring your presence to us which no malice can prevent, nor any obstacle hinder; then do not, I beseech you, allow any negligence to hold you back.

You wrote your friend a long letter of consolation, prompted no doubt by his misfortunes, but really telling of your own. The detailed account you gave of these may have been intended for his comfort, but it also greatly increased our own feeling of desolation; in your desire to heal his wounds you have dealt us fresh wounds of grief as well as re-opening the old. I beg you, then, as you set about tending the wounds which others have dealt, heal the wounds you have yourself inflicted. You have done your duty to a friend and comrade, discharged your debt to friendship and comradeship, but you have bound yourself by a greater debt to us who can properly be called not friends so much as dearest friends, not comrades but daughters, or any other conceivable name more tender and holy. How great the debt by which you have bound yourself to us needs neither proof nor witness, were it in any doubt; if everyone kept silent, the facts themselves would cry out. For you after God are the sole founder of this place, the sole builder of this oratory, the sole creator of this community. You have built nothing here upon another man's foundation. Everything here is your own creation. This was a wilderness open to wild beasts and brigands, a place which had known no home nor habitation of men. In the very lairs of wild beasts and lurking-places of robbers, where the name of God was never heard, you built a sanctuary to God and dedicated a shrine in the name of the Holy Spirit. To build it you drew nothing from the riches of kings and princes, though their wealth was great and could have been yours for the asking: whatever was done, the credit was to be yours alone. Clerks and scholars came flocking here, eager for your teaching, and ministered to all your needs; and even those who had lived on the benefices of the Church and knew only how to receive offerings, not to make them, whose hands were held out to take but not to give, became pressing in their lavish offers of assistance.

And so it is yours, truly your own, this new plantation for God's purpose, but it is sown with plants which are still very tender and need watering if they are to thrive. Through its feminine nature this plantation would be weak and frail even if it were not new; and so it needs a more careful and regular cultivation, according to the words of the Apostle: 'I planted the

seed and Apollos watered it; but God made it grow.'
The Apostle through the doctrine that he preached had
planted and established in the faith the Corinthians, to
whom he was writing. Afterwards the Apostle's own
disciple, Apollos, had watered them with his holy
exhortations and so God's grace bestowed on them
growth in the virtues. You cultivate a vineyard of
another's vines which you did not plant yourself and
which has now turned to bitterness against you, so that
often your advice brings no result and your holy words
are uttered in vain. You devote your care to another's
vineyard; think what you owe to your own. You teach
and admonish rebels to no purpose, and in vain you
cast pearls of divine eloquence before swine. While
you spend so much on the stubborn, consider what you
owe to the obedient; you are so generous to your
enemies but should reflect on how you are indebted to
your daughters. Apart from everything else, consider
the close tie by which you have bound yourself to me,
and repay the debt you owe a whole community of
devoted women by discharging it the more dutifully to
her who is yours alone.

Your superior wisdom knows better than our humble
learning of the many serious treatises which the holy
Fathers compiled for the instruction or exhortation or
even the consolation of holy women, and of the care
with which these were composed. And so in the pre-
carious early days of our conversion long ago I was not
a little surprised and troubled by your forgetfulness,
when neither reverence for God nor our mutual love
nor the example of the holy Fathers made you think of

trying to comfort me, wavering and exhausted as I was by prolonged grief, either by word when I was with you or by letter when we had parted. Yet you must know that you are bound to me by an obligation which is all the greater for the further close tie of the marriage sacrament uniting us, and are the deeper in my debt because of the love I have always borne you, as everyone knows, a love which is beyond all bounds.

You know, beloved, as everyone knows, how much I have lost in you, how at one wretched stroke of fortune that supreme act of flagrant treachery robbed me of my very self in robbing me of you; and how my sorrow for my loss is nothing compared with what I feel for the manner in which I lost you. Surely the greater the cause for grief the greater the need for the help of consolation, and this no one can bring but you; you are the sole cause of my sorrow, and you alone can grant me the grace of consolation. You alone have the power to make me sad, to bring me happiness or comfort; you alone have so great a debt to repay me, particularly now when I have carried out all your orders so implicitly that when I was powerless to oppose you in anything, I found strength at your command to destroy myself. I did more, strange to say – my love rose to such heights of madness that it robbed itself of what it most desired beyond hope of recovery, when immediately at your bidding I changed my clothing along with my mind, in order to prove you the sole possessor of my body and my will alike.

God knows I never sought anything in you except yourself; I wanted simply you, nothing of yours. I looked for no marriage-bond, no marriage portion, and it was not my own pleasures and wishes I sought to gratify, as you well know, but yours. The name of wife may seem more sacred or more binding, but sweeter for me will always be the word friend [*amica*], or, if you will permit me, that of concubine or whore. I believed that the more I humbled myself on your account, the more gratitude I should win from you, and also the less damage I should do to the brightness of your reputation.

You yourself on your own account did not altogether forget this in the letter of consolation I have spoken of which you wrote to a friend; there you thought fit to set out some of the reasons I gave in trying to dissuade you from binding us together in an ill-starred marriage. But you kept silent about most of my arguments for preferring love to wedlock and freedom to chains. God is my witness that if Augustus, Emperor of the whole world, thought fit to honour me with marriage and conferred all the earth on me to possess for ever, it would be dearer and more honourable to me to be called not his Empress but your whore.

For a person's worth does not rest on wealth or power; these depend on fortune, but worth on its merits. And a woman should realize that if she marries a rich man more readily than a poor one, and desires her husband more for his possessions than for himself, she is offering herself for sale. Certainly any woman who comes to marry through desires of this kind deserves wages, not gratitude, for clearly her mind is on the man's property, not himself, and she would be ready to prostitute herself to a richer man, if she could. This is evident from the argument put forward, in the dialogue of Aeschines Socraticus, by the philosopher Aspasia to Xenophon and his wife. When she had expounded it in an effort to bring about a reconciliation between them, this philosopher ended with these words: 'Unless you come to believe that there is no better man nor worthier woman on earth you will always still be looking for what you judge the best thing of all – to be the husband of the best of wives and the wife of the best of husbands.'

These are saintly words which are more than philosophic; indeed, they deserve the name of wisdom, not philosophy. It is a holy error and a blessed delusion between man and wife that perfect love can keep the ties of marriage unbroken not so much through bodily continence as chastity of spirit. But what error permitted other women, plain truth permitted me, and what they thought of their husbands, the world in general believed, or rather, knew to be true of yourself; so that my love for you was the more genuine for being further removed from error. What king or philosopher could match your fame? What district, town or village did not long to see you? When you appeared in public, who – I ask – did not hurry to catch a glimpse of you, or crane her neck and strain her eyes to follow your departure? Every wife, every young girl desired you in absence and was on fire in your presence; queens and great ladies envied me my joys and my bed.

In you, I readily admit, there were two things especially, with which you could immediately win the heart of any woman – the gift of composing and the gift of singing. We know that the other philosophers achieved no success in these things, whereas for you they served as a kind of game, as a recreation from the labour and exertion of philosophy. You have left many songs composed in amatory verse or rhyme. Because of the great sweetness of their poetry as much as of their tunes, they have been frequently sung and they kept your name unceasingly on everyone's lips. The beauty of the melodies ensured that even those who knew no Latin did not forget you; more than anything this made women sigh for love of you. And as most of these songs told of our love, they soon made me widely known and roused the envy of many women against me. For your manhood was adorned by every grace of mind and body, and among the women who envied me then, could there be one now who does not feel compelled by my misfortune to sympathize with my loss of such joys? Who is there who was once my enemy, whether man or woman, who is not moved now by the compassion which is my due? Wholly guilty though I am, I am also, as you know, wholly innocent. It is not the deed but the intention of the doer which makes the crime, and justice should weigh not what was done but the spirit in which it is done. What my intention towards you has always been, you alone who have known it can judge. I submit all to your scrutiny, yield to your testimony in all things.

Tell me one thing, if you can. Why, after our entry into religion, which was your decision alone, have I been so neglected and forgotten by you that I have neither a word from you when you are here to give me strength nor the consolation of a letter in absence? Tell me, I say, if you can – or I will tell you what I think and indeed everyone suspects. It was desire, not affection which bound you to me, the flame of lust rather than love. So when the end came to what you desired, any show of feeling you used to make went with it. This is not merely my own opinion, beloved, it is everyone's. There is nothing personal or private about it; it is the general view which is widely held. I only wish that it *were* mine alone, and that the love you professed could find someone to defend it and so comfort me in my grief for a while. I wish I could think of some explanation which would excuse you and somehow cover up the way you hold me cheap.

I beg you then to listen to what I ask – you will see that it is a small favour which you can easily grant. While I am denied your presence, give me at least through your words – of which you have enough and to spare – some sweet semblance of yourself. It is no use my hoping for generosity in deeds if you are grudging in words. Up to now I had thought I deserved much of you, seeing that I carried out everything for your sake and continue up to the present moment in complete obedience to you. It was not any sense of vocation which brought me as a young girl to accept the austerities of the cloister, but your bidding alone, and if I deserve no gratitude from you, you may judge for yourself how my labours are in vain. I can expect no reward for this from God, for it is certain that I have done nothing as yet for love of him. When you hurried towards God I followed you, indeed, I went first to take the veil – perhaps you were thinking how Lot's wife turned back when you made me put on the religious habit and take my vows before you gave yourself to God. Your lack of trust in me over this one thing, I confess, overwhelmed me with grief and shame. I would have had no hesitation, God knows, in following you or going ahead at your bidding to the flames of Hell. My heart was not in me but with you, and now, even more, if it is not with you it is nowhere; truly, without you it cannot exist. See that it fares well with you, I beg, as it will if it finds you kind, if you give grace in return for grace, small for great, words for deeds. If only your love had less confidence in me, my dear, so that you would be more concerned on my behalf! But as it is, the more I have made you feel secure in me, the more I have to bear with your neglect.

Remember, I implore you, what I have done, and think how much you owe me. While I enjoyed with you the pleasures of the flesh, many were uncertain whether I was prompted by love or lust; but now the end is proof of the beginning. I have finally denied myself every pleasure in obedience to your will, kept nothing for myself except to prove that now, even more, I am yours. Consider then your injustice, if when I deserve more you give me less, or rather, nothing at all, especially when it is a small thing I ask of you and one you could so easily grant. And so, in the name of that God to whom you have dedicated yourself, I beg you to restore your presence to me in the way you can – by writing me some word of comfort, so that in this at least I may find increased strength and readiness to serve God. When in the past you sought me out for sinful pleasures your letters came to me thick and fast, and your many songs put your Heloise on everyone's lips, so that every street and house resounded with my name. Is it not far better now to summon me to God than it was then to satisfy our lust? I beg you, think what you owe me, give ear to my pleas, and I will finish a long letter with a brief ending: farewell, my only love.

LETTER 3

Abelard to Heloise: Loving the Living

If since our conversion from the world to God I have not yet written you any word of comfort or advice, it must not be attributed to indifference on my part but to your own good sense, in which I have always had such confidence that I did not think anything was needed; God's grace has bestowed on you all essentials to enable you to instruct the erring, comfort the weak and encourage the faint-hearted, both by word and example, as, indeed, you have been doing since you first held the office of prioress under your abbess. So if you still watch over your daughters as carefully as you did previously over your sisters, it is sufficient to make me believe that any teaching or exhortation from me would now be wholly superfluous. If, on the other hand, in your humility you think differently, and you feel that you have need of my instruction and writings in matters pertaining to God, write to me what you want, so that I may answer as God permits me. Meanwhile thanks be to God who has filled all your hearts with anxiety for my desperate, unceasing perils, and made you share in my affliction; may divine mercy protect me through the support of your prayers and quickly crush Satan beneath our feet. To this end in particular, I hasten to send the Psalter you earnestly begged from me, my sister once dear in the world and now dearest in Christ, so that you may offer a perpetual sacrifice of prayers to the Lord for our many great aberrations, and for the dangers which daily threaten me.

We have indeed many examples as evidence of the high position in the eyes of God and his saints which has been won by the prayers of the faithful, especially those of women on behalf of their dear ones and of wives for their husbands. The Apostle observes this closely when he bids us pray continually. We read that the Lord said to Moses 'Let me alone, to vent my anger upon them,' and to Jeremiah 'Therefore offer no prayer for these people nor stand in my path.' By these words the Lord himself makes it clear that the prayers of the devout set a kind of bridle on his wrath and check it from raging against sinners as fully as they deserve; just as a man who is willingly moved by his sense of justice to take vengeance can be turned aside by the entreaties of his friends and forcibly restrained, as it were, against his will. Thus when the Lord says to one who is praying or about to pray, 'Let me alone and do not stand in my path,' he forbids prayers to be offered to him on behalf of the impious; yet the just man prays though the Lord forbids, obtains his requests and alters the sentence of the angry judge. And so the passage about Moses continues: 'And the Lord repented and spared his people the evil with which he had threatened them.' Elsewhere it is written about the universal works of God, 'He spoke, and it was.' But in this passage it is also recorded that he had said the people deserved affliction, but he had been prevented by the power of prayer from carrying out his words.

Consider then the great power of prayer, if we pray as we are bidden, seeing that the prophet won by prayer what he was forbidden to pray for, and turned God aside from his declared intention. And another prophet says to God: 'In thy wrath remember mercy.' The lords of the earth should listen and take note, for they are found obstinate rather than just in the execution of the justice they have decreed and pronounced; they blush to appear lax if they are merciful, and untruthful if they change a pronouncement or do not carry out a decision which lacked foresight, even if they can emend their words by their actions. Such men could properly be compared with Jephtha, who made a foolish vow and in carrying it out even more foolishly, killed his only daughter. But he who desires to be a 'member of his body' says with the Psalmist 'I will sing of mercy and justice unto thee, O Lord.' Mercy, it is written, exalts judgement, in accordance with the threat elsewhere in the Scriptures: 'In that judgement there will be no mercy for the man who has shown no mercy.' The Psalmist himself considered this carefully when, at the entreaty of the wife of Nabal the Carmelite, as an act of mercy he broke the oath he had justly sworn concerning her husband and the destruction of his house. Thus he set prayer above justice, and the man's wrong-doing was wiped out by the entreaties of his wife.

Here you have an example, sister, and an assurance

how much your prayers for me may prevail on God, if this woman's did so much for her husband, seeing that God who is our father loves his children more than David did a suppliant woman. David was indeed considered a pious and merciful man, but God is piety and mercy itself. And the woman whose entreaties David heard then was an ordinary lay person, in no way bound to God by the profession of holy devotion; whereas if you alone are not enough to win an answer to your prayer, the holy convent of widows and virgins which is with you will succeed where you cannot by yourself. For when the Truth says to the disciples, 'When two or three have met together in my name, I am there among them,' and again, 'If two of you agree about any request you have to make, it shall be granted by my Father,' we can all see how the communal prayer of a holy congregation must prevail upon God. If, as the apostle James says, 'A good man's prayer is powerful and effective,' what should we hope for from the large numbers of a holy congregation? You know, dearest sister, from the thirty-eighth homily of St Gregory how much support the prayers of his fellow brethren quickly brought a brother, although he was unwilling and resisted. The depths of his misery, the fear of peril which tormented his unhappy soul, the utter despair and weariness of life which made him try to call his brethren from their prayers – all the details set out there cannot have escaped your understanding.

May this example give you and your convent of holy sisters greater confidence in prayer, so that I may be preserved alive for you all, through him, from whom, as Paul bears witness, women have even received back their dead raised to life. For if you turn the pages of the Old and New Testaments you will find that the greatest miracles of resurrection were shown only, or mostly, to women, and were performed for them or on them. The Old Testament records two instances of men raised from the dead at the entreaties of their mothers, by Elijah and his disciple Elisha. The Gospel, it is true, has three instances only of the dead being raised by the Lord but, as they were shown to women only, they provide factual confirmation of the Apostle's words I quoted above: 'Women received back their dead raised to life.' It was to a widow at the gate of the city of Nain that the Lord restored her son, moved by compassion for her, and he also raised Lazarus his own friend at the entreaty of his sisters Mary and Martha. And when he granted this same favour to the daughter of the ruler of the synagogue at her father's petition, again 'women received back their dead raised to life,' for in being brought back to life she received her own body from death just as those other women received the bodies of their dead.

Now these resurrections were performed with only a few interceding; and so the multiplied prayers of your shared devotion should easily win the preservation of my own life. The more God is pleased by the abstinence and continence which women have dedicated to him, the more willing he will be to grant their prayers. Moreover, it may well be that the majority of those raised from the dead were not of the faith, for we do not read that the widow mentioned above whose son was raised without her asking was a believer. But in our case we are bound together by the integrity of our faith and united in our profession of the same religious life.

Let me now pass from the holy convent of your community, where so many virgins and widows are dedicated to continual service of the Lord, and come to you alone, you whose sanctity must surely have the greatest influence in the eyes of God, and who are bound to do everything possible on my behalf, especially now when I am in the toils of such adversity. Always remember then in your prayers him who is especially yours; watch and pray the more confidently as you recognize your cause is just, and so more acceptable to him to whom you pray. Listen, I beg you, with the ear of your heart to what you have so often heard with your bodily ear. In the book of Proverbs it is written that 'A capable wife is her husband's crown,' and again, 'Find a wife and you find a good thing; so you will earn the favour of the Lord'; yet again, 'Home and wealth may come down from ancestors; but an intelligent wife is a gift from the Lord.' In Ecclesiasticus too it says that 'A good wife makes a happy husband,' and a little later, 'A good wife means a good life.' And we have it on the Apostle's authority that 'the unbelieving husband now belongs to God through his wife'. A special instance of this was granted by God's grace in our own country of France, when Clovis the king was converted to the Christian faith more by the prayers of his wife than by the preaching of holy men; his entire kingdom was then placed under divine law so that humbler men should be encouraged by the

am gripped by fear of greater peril. And so I ask of you in entreaty, and entreat you in asking, particularly now that I am absent from you, to show me how truly your charity extends to the absent by adding this form of special prayer at the conclusion of each hour:

RESPONSE: O Lord, Father and Ruler of my life, do not desert me, lest I fall before my adversaries and my enemy gloats over me.

VERSICLE: Grasp shield and buckler and rise up to help me, lest my enemy gloats.

PRAYER: Save thy servant, O my God, whose hope is in thee. Send him help, O Lord, from thy holy place, and watch over him from Zion. Be a tower of strength to him, O Lord, in the face of his enemy. Lord hear my prayer, and let my cry for help reach thee.

(LET US PRAY) O God, who through thy servant hast been pleased to gather together thy hand-maidens in thy name, we beseech thee to protect him in all adversity and restore him in safety to thy handmaidens. Through our Lord, etc.

But if the Lord shall deliver me into the hands of my enemies so that they overcome and kill me, or by whatever chance I enter upon the way of all flesh while absent from you, wherever my body may lie, buried or unburied, I beg you to have it brought to your burial-ground, where our daughters, or rather, our sisters in Christ may see my tomb more often and thereby be encouraged to pour out their prayers more

77

fully to the Lord on my behalf. There is no place, I think, so safe and salutary for a soul grieving for its sins and desolated by its transgressions than that which is specially consecrated to the true Paraclete, the Comforter, and which is particularly designated by his name. Nor do I believe that there is any place more fitting for Christian burial among the faithful than one amongst women dedicated to Christ. Women were concerned for the tomb of our Lord Jesus Christ, they came ahead and followed after, bringing precious ointments, keeping close watch around this tomb, weeping for the death of the Bridegroom, as it is written: 'The women sitting at the tomb wept and lamented for the Lord.' And there they were first reassured about his resurrection by the appearance of an angel and the words he spoke to them; later on they were found worthy both to taste the joy of his resurrection when he twice appeared to them, and also to touch him with their hands.

Finally, I ask this of you above all else: at present you are over-anxious about the danger to my body, but then your chief concern must be for the salvation of my soul, and you must show the dead man how much you loved the living by the special support of prayers chosen for him.

Live, fare you well, yourself and your sisters with you,

Live, but I pray, in Christ be mindful of me.

LETTER 4

Heloise to Abelard: Forbidden Pleasures

I am surprised, my only love, that contrary to custom in letterwriting and, indeed, to the natural order, you have thought fit to put my name before yours in the greeting which heads your letter, so that we have the woman before the man, wife before husband, handmaid before lord, nun before monk, deaconess before priest and abbess before abbot. Surely the right and proper order is for those who write to their superiors or equals to put their names before their own, but in letters to inferiors, precedence in order of address follows precedence in rank.

We were also greatly surprised when instead of bringing us the healing balm of comfort as you should have, you increased our desolation and made the tears to flow which you should have dried. For which of us could remain dry-eyed on hearing the words you wrote towards the end of your letter: 'But if the Lord shall deliver me into the hands of my enemies so that they overcome and kill me . . .'? My dearest, how could you think such a thought? How could you give voice to it? Never may God be so forgetful of his humble handmaids as to let them outlive you; never may he grant us a life which would be harder to bear than any form of death. The proper course would be for you to perform our funeral rites, for you to commend our souls to God, and to send ahead of you those whom you assembled for God's service – so that you need no longer be troubled by worries for us, and follow after us the more gladly because freed from concern for our salvation. Spare us, I implore you, my lord, spare us words such as these which can only intensify our existing unhappiness; do not deny us, before death, the one thing by which we live. 'Sufficient unto the day is the evil thereof,' and that day, shrouded in bitterness, will bring with it distress enough to all it comes upon. 'Why is it necessary,' says Seneca, 'to summon up evil' and to destroy life before death?

You ask us, my only one, if you chance to die when absent from us, to have your body brought to our burial-ground so that you may reap a fuller harvest from the prayers we shall offer in constant memory of you. But how could you suppose that our memory of you could ever fade? Besides, what time will there be then which will be fitting for prayer, when extreme distress will allow us no peace, when the soul will lose its power of reason and the tongue its use of speech? Or when the frantic mind, far from being resigned, may even (if I may say so) rage against God himself, and provoke him with complaints instead of placating him with prayers? In our misery then we shall have time only for tears and no power to pray; we shall be hurrying to follow, not to bury you, so that we may share your grave instead of laying you in it. If we lose our life in you, we shall not be able to go on living

when you leave us. I would not even have us live to see
that day, for if the mere mention of your death is death
for us, what will the reality be if it finds us still alive?
God grant we may never live on to perform this duty,
to render you the service which we look for from you
alone; in this may we go before, not after you!

And so, I beg you, spare us – spare her at least, who
is your only one – by refraining from words like these.
They pierce our hearts with swords of death, so that
what comes before is more painful than death itself. A
heart which is exhausted with grief cannot find peace,
nor can a mind preoccupied with anxieties genuinely
devote itself to God. I beseech you not to hinder God's
service to which you specially committed us. Whatever
has to come to us bringing with it total grief we must
hope will come suddenly, without torturing us far in
advance with useless apprehension which no foresight
can relieve. This is what the poet has in mind when he
prays to God:

> May it be sudden, whatever you plan for us; may man's
>   mind
> Be blind to the future. Let him hope on in his fears.

But if I lose you, what is left for me to hope for?
What reason for continuing on life's pilgrimage, for
which I have no support but you, and none in you
save the knowledge that you are alive, now that I am
forbidden all other pleasures in you and denied even
the joy of your presence which from time to time could
restore me to myself? O God – if it is lawful to say it

– cruel to me in everything! O merciless mercy! O Fortune who is only ill-fortune, who has already spent on me so many of the shafts she uses in her battle against mankind that she has none left with which to vent her anger on others. She has emptied a full quiver on me, so that henceforth no one else need fear her onslaughts, and if she still had a single arrow she could find no place in me to take a wound. Her only dread is that through my many wounds death may end my sufferings; and though she does not cease to destroy me, she still fears the destruction which she hurries on.

Of all wretched women I am the most wretched, and amongst the unhappy I am unhappiest. The higher I was exalted when you preferred me to all other women, the greater my suffering over my own fall and yours, when equally I was flung down; for the higher the ascent, the heavier the fall. Has Fortune ever set any great or noble woman above me or made her my equal, only to be similarly cast down and crushed with grief? What glory she gave me in you, what ruin she brought upon me through you! Violent in either extreme, she showed no moderation in good or evil. To make me the saddest of all women she first made me blessed above all, so that when I thought how much I had lost, my consuming grief would match my crushing loss, and my sorrow for what was taken from me would be the greater for the fuller joy of possession which had gone before; and so that the happiness of supreme ecstasy would end in the supreme bitterness of sorrow.

Moreover, to add to my indignation at the outrage, all the laws of equity in our case were reversed. For while we enjoyed the pleasures of an uneasy love and abandoned ourselves to fornication (if I may use an ugly but expressive word) we were spared God's severity. But when we amended our unlawful conduct by what was lawful, and atoned for the shame of fornication by an honourable marriage, then the Lord in his anger laid his hand heavily upon us, and would not permit a chaste union though he had long tolerated one which was unchaste. The punishment you suffered would have been proper vengeance for men caught in open adultery. But what others deserve for adultery came upon you through a marriage which you believed had made amends for all previous wrongdoing; what adulterous women have brought upon their lovers, your own wife brought on you. Nor was this at the time when we abandoned ourselves to our former delights, but when we had already parted and were living more chastely, you presiding over the school in Paris and I at your command living with the nuns at Argenteuil. Thus we were separated, to give you more time to devote yourself to your pupils, and me more freedom for prayer and meditation on the Scriptures, both of us leading a life which was more holy as well as more chaste. It was then that you alone paid the penalty in your body for what we had both done equally. You alone were punished though we were both to blame, and you paid all, though you had deserved less, for you had made more than necessary reparation by humbling yourself on my account and had raised me and all my

83

kind to your own level – so much less then, in the eyes
of God and of your betrayers, should you have been
thought deserving of such punishment.

What misery for me – born as I was to be the cause
of such a crime! Is it the general lot of women to bring
total ruin on great men? Hence the warning about
women in Proverbs: 'But now, my son, listen to me,
attend to what I say: do not let your heart entice you
into her ways, do not stray down her paths; she has
wounded and laid low so many, and the strongest have
all been her victims. Her house is the way to hell, and
leads down to the halls of death.' And in Ecclesiastes:
'I put all to the test . . . I find woman more bitter than
death; she is a snare, her heart a net, her arms are
chains. He who is pleasing to God eludes her, but the
sinner is her captive.'

It was the first woman in the beginning who lured
man from Paradise, and she who had been created
by the Lord as his helpmate became the instrument of
his total downfall. And that mighty man of the Lord,
[Samson] the Nazirite whose conception was an-
nounced by an angel, Delilah alone overcame; betrayed
to his enemies and robbed of his sight, he was driven by
his suffering to destroy himself along with his enemies.
Only the woman he had had sex with could infatuate
Solomon, wisest of all men; she drove him to such a
pitch of madness that although he was the man whom
the Lord had chosen to build the temple in preference
to his father David, who was a righteous man, she
plunged him into idolatry until the end of his life, so
that he abandoned the worship of God which he had

84

preached and taught in word and writing. Job, holiest of men, fought his last and hardest battle against his wife, who urged him to curse God. The cunning arch-tempter well knew from repeated experience that men are most easily brought to ruin through their wives, and so he directed his usual malice against us too, and tempted you through marriage when he could not destroy you through fornication. Denied the power to do evil through evil, he effected evil through good.

At least I can thank God for this: the tempter did not prevail on me to do wrong of my own consent, like the women I have mentioned, though in the outcome he made me the instrument of his malice. But even if my conscience is clear through innocence, and no consent of mine makes me guilty of this crime, too many earlier sins were committed to allow me to be wholly free from guilt. I yielded long before to the pleasures of carnal desires, and merited then what I weep for now. The sequel is a fitting punishment for my former sins, and an evil beginning must be expected to come to a bad end. For this offence, above all, may I have strength to do proper penance, so that at least by long contrition I can make some amends for your pain from the wound inflicted on you; and what you suffered in the body for a time, I may suffer, as is right, throughout my life in contrition of mind, and thus make reparation to you at least, if not to God.

For if I truthfully admit to the weakness of my most wretched soul, I can find no penitence whereby to appease God, whom I always accuse of the greatest cruelty in regard to this outrage. By rebelling against his ordinance, I offend him more by my indignation than I placate him by making amends through penitence. How can it be called repentance for sins, however great the mortification of the flesh, if the mind still retains the will to sin and is on fire with its old desires? It is easy enough for anyone to confess his sins, to accuse himself, or even to mortify his body in outward show of penance, but it is very difficult to tear the heart away from hankering after its dearest pleasures. Quite rightly then, when the saintly Job said, 'I will speak out against myself,' that is, 'I will loose my tongue and open my mouth in confession to accuse myself of my sins,' he added at once, 'I will speak out in bitterness of soul.' St Gregory comments on this: 'There are some who confess their faults aloud but in doing so do not know how to groan over them – they speak cheerfully of what should be lamented. And so whoever hates his faults and confesses them must still confess them in bitterness of spirit, so that this bitterness may punish him for what his tongue, at his mind's bidding, accuses him.' But this bitterness of true repentance is very rare, as St Ambrose observes, when he says: 'I have more easily found men who have preserved their innocence than men who have known repentance.'

In my case, the pleasures of lovers which we shared have been too sweet – they cannot displease me, and can scarcely shift from my memory. Wherever I turn they are always there before my eyes, bringing with them awakened longings and fantasies which will not even let me sleep. Even during the celebration of the

Mass, when our prayers should be purer, lewd visions of those pleasures take such a hold upon my unhappy soul that my thoughts are on their wantonness instead of on prayers. I should be groaning over the sins I have committed, but I can only sigh for what I have lost. Everything we did and also the times and places where we did it are stamped on my heart along with your image, so that I live through them all again with you. Even in sleep I know no respite. Sometimes my thoughts are betrayed in a movement of my body, or they break out in an unguarded word. In my utter wretchedness, that cry from a suffering soul could well be mine: 'Miserable creature that I am, who is there to rescue me out of the body doomed to this death?' Would that I could truthfully answer: 'The grace of God through Jesus Christ our Lord.' This grace, my dearest, came upon you unsought – a single wound of the body by freeing you from these torments has healed many wounds in your soul. Where God may seem to you an adversary, he has in fact proved himself kind: like an honest doctor who does not shrink from giving pain if it will bring about a cure. But for me, youth and passion and experience of pleasures which were so delightful intensify the torments of the flesh and longings of desire, and the assault is the more over-whelming as the nature they attack is the weaker.

Men call me chaste; they do not know the hypocrite I am. They consider purity of the flesh a virtue, though virtue belongs not to the body but to the soul. I can win praise in the eyes of men but deserve none before God, who searches our hearts and loins and sees in our darkness. I am judged religious at a time when there is little in religion which is not hypocrisy, when whoever does not offend the opinions of men receives the highest praise. And yet perhaps there is some merit and it seems somehow acceptable to God, if a person whatever her intention gives no offence to the Church in her outward behaviour, if the name of the Lord is not blasphemed among the infidels because of her nor if she does not disgrace the Order of her profession amongst the worldly. And this too is a gift of God's grace and comes through his bounty – not only to do good but to abstain from evil – though the latter is vain if the former does not follow from it, as it is written: 'Turn from evil and do good.' Both are vain if not done for love of God.

At every stage of my life up to now, as God knows, I have feared to offend you rather than God, and tried to please you more than him. It was your command, not love of God, which made me take the veil. Look at the unhappy life I lead, pitiable beyond any other, if in this world I must endure so much in vain, with no hope of future reward. For a long time my pretence deceived you, as it did many, so that you mistook hypocrisy for piety; and therefore you commend yourself to our prayers and ask me for what I expect from you. I beg you, do not feel so sure of me that you cease to help me by your own prayers. Do not suppose me healthy and so withdraw the grace of your healing. Do not believe I want for nothing and delay helping me in my hour of need. Do not think me strong, lest I fall before you can sustain me. False praise has harmed many and taken from them the support they needed. The Lord cries out through Isaiah: 'O my people! Those who call you happy lead you astray and confuse the path you should take.' And through Ezekiel he says: 'Woe to them that sew cushions under every elbow and make pillows for the heads of people of every age in order to catch souls.' On the other hand, through Solomon it is said that 'The sayings of the wise are sharp as goads, like nails driven home.' That is to say, nails which cannot touch wounds gently, but only pierce through them.

Cease praising me, I beg you, lest you acquire the base stigma of being a flatterer or the charge of telling lies, or the breath of my vanity blows away any merit you saw in me to praise. No one with medical knowledge diagnoses an internal illness by examining only outward appearance. What is common to the damned and the elect can win no favour in the eyes of God: of such a kind are the outward actions which are performed more eagerly by hypocrites than by saints. 'The heart of man is deceitful and inscrutable; who can fathom it?' And: 'A road may seem straightforward to a man, yet may end as the way to death.' It is rash for man to pass judgement on what is reserved for God's scrutiny, and so it is also written: 'Do not praise a man in his lifetime.' By this is meant, do not praise a man while in doing so you can make him no longer praiseworthy.

To me your praise is the more dangerous because I welcome it. The more anxious I am to please you in everything, the more I am won over and delighted by it. I beg you, be fearful for me always, instead of feeling confidence in me, so that I may always find help in your solicitude. Now particularly you should fear, now when I no longer have in you an outlet for my incontinence. I do not wish you to exhort me to virtue or summon me to battle. You say: 'Power comes to its full strength in weakness' and 'He cannot win a crown unless he has kept the rules.' I do not seek a crown of victory; it is sufficient for me to avoid danger, and this is safer than engaging in war. In whatever corner of heaven God shall place me, it will be enough for me. No one will envy one another there, and what each one has will suffice. So that I might add the strength of authority to this our counsel, let us hear St Jerome: 'I confess my weakness, I do not wish to fight in hope of victory, lest the day comes when I lose the battle. What need is there to forsake what is certain and pursue uncertainty?'

more attentively on the subject of your own pleas as you find me less to blame in my own and be less ready to refuse me when you see me less deserving of reproach.

What you call the unnatural order of my greeting, if you consider it carefully, was in accordance with your own view as well as mine. For it is common knowledge, as you yourself have shown, that in writing to superiors one puts their name first, and you must realize that you became my superior from the day when you began to be my lady on becoming the bride of my Lord; witness St Jerome, who writes to Eustochium 'This is my reason for writing "my lady Eustochium". Surely I must address as "my lady" her who is the bride of my Lord.' It was a fortunate trading of your married state: as you were previously the wife of a poor mortal and now you are raised to the bed of the high king. By the privilege of this honour you are set not only over your former husband but over every servant of that king. So you should not be surprised if I commend myself in life as in death to the prayers of your community, seeing that in common law it is accepted that wives are better able than their households to intercede with their husbands, being ladies rather than servants. As an illustration of this, the Psalmist says of the queen and bride of the high king: 'On your right stands the queen,' as if it were clearly stated that she is nearest to her husband and closest to his side, and proceeds as an equal, while all the rest stand apart or follow behind. The bride in the Canticles, an Ethiopian (such as the one Moses took as a wife) rejoices in the glory of her privileged position and says: 'I am black but lovely, daughters of Jerusalem; therefore the king has loved me and brought me into his chamber.' And again, 'Take no notice of my darkness, because the sun has discoloured me.' Allegorically it is the contemplative soul which is described in these words and specifically called the bride of Christ. Your outer habit indicates that these words have particular application to you. For your outer garb of coarse black clothing, like the mourning worn by good widows who weep for the dead husbands they had loved, shows you to be, in the words of the Apostle, truly widowed and desolate and such as the Church should be charged to support. The Scriptures also record the grief of these widows for their spouse who was slain, in the words: 'The women sitting at the tomb wept and lamented for the Lord.'

The Ethiopian woman is black in the outer part of her flesh and as regards exterior appearance looks less lovely than other women; yet she is not unlike them within, but in several respects she is whiter and lovelier, in her bones, for instance, or her teeth. Indeed, whiteness of teeth is also praised in the bridegroom, in reference to 'his teeth whiter than milk'. And so she is black outside but lovely within; for she is blackened outside in the flesh because in this life she suffers bodily affliction through the repeated tribulations of adversity, according to the saying of the Apostle: 'Persecution will come to all who want to live a godly life as Christians.' As prosperity is marked by white, so adversity may properly be indicated by black, and she is white within in her bones because her soul is strong in virtues, as it is written that 'All the glory of the king's daughter is within.' For the bones within, surrounded by the flesh without, are the strength and support of the very flesh they wear or sustain, and can properly stand for the soul which gives life and sustenance to the flesh itself in which it is, and to which it gives movement and direction and provision for all its well-being. Its whiteness or beauty is the sum of the virtues which adorn it.

She is black too in outward things because while she is still an exile on life's pilgrimage, she keeps herself humble and abject in this life so that she may be exalted in the next, where she is hidden with Christ in God, once she has reached her homeland. So indeed the true sun changes her colour because the heavenly love of the bridegroom humbles her like this, or torments her with tribulations lest prosperity raises her up. He changes her colour, that is, he makes her different from other women who thirst for earthly things and seek worldly glory, so that she may truly become through her humility a lily of the valley, and not a lily of the heights like those foolish virgins who pride themselves on purity of the flesh or an outward show of self-denial, and then wither in the fire of temptation. And she rightly told the daughters of Jerusalem, that is, the weaker amongst the faithful who deserve to be called daughters rather than sons, 'Take no notice of my darkness, because the sun has discoloured me.' She might say more openly: 'The fact that I humble myself in this way or bear adversity so bravely is due to no virtue of mine but to the grace of him whom I serve.'

This is not the way of heretics and hypocrites who (at any rate when others are present) humiliate themselves to excess in hopes of earthly glory, and endure much to no purpose. The sort of abjection or tribulation they put up with is indeed surprising, and they are the most pitiable of men, enjoying the good things neither of this life nor of the life to come. It is with this in mind that the bride says, 'Do not wonder that I do so'; but we must wonder at those who vainly burn with desire for worldly praise and deny themselves advantages on earth so that they are as unhappy in their present life as they will be in the next. Such self-denial is that of the foolish virgins who found the door shut against them.

And she did well to say that, because she is black, as we said, and lovely, she is chosen and taken into the king's bedchamber, that is, to that secret place of peace and contemplation, and into the bed, of which she says elsewhere, 'Night after night on my bed I have sought my true love.' Indeed, the disfigurement of her blackness makes her love what is hidden rather than open, what is secret rather than public. Such a wife desires private, not public delights with her husband, and would rather be experienced in bed than seen at table. Moreover it often happens that the flesh of black women is all the softer to touch though it is less attractive to look at, and for this reason the pleasure they give is greater and more suitable for private than for public gratification. Their husbands take them into a bedroom to enjoy them rather than parade them in public. Following this metaphor, when that spiritual bride said, 'I am black but lovely,' she rightly added at once, 'Therefore the king has loved me and brought me into his chamber.' She relates each point to the other: because she was lovely he loved her, and because she was black he brought her into his chamber. She is lovely, as we said before, with virtues within which the bridegroom loves, and black outside from the adversity of bodily tribulation. Such blackness of bodily tribulation easily turns the minds of the faithful away from love of earthly things and attaches them to the desire for eternal life, often leading them from the stormy life of the world to retirement for contemplation. Thus St Jerome writes that our own, that is, the monastic life, took its beginning from Paul [of Thebes].

The humiliation of coarse garments also looks to retirement rather than to public life, and is to be preserved as being most suitable for the life of humility and withdrawal which especially befits our profession. The greatest encouragement to public display is costly clothing, which is sought by none except for empty display and worldly ceremony, as St Gregory clearly shows in saying that 'No one adorns himself in private, only where he can be seen.' As for the chamber of the bride, it is the one to which the bridegroom himself in the Gospel invites anyone who prays, saying 'But when you pray, go into a room by yourself, shut the door and pray to your Father.' He could have added 'not like the hypocrites, at street corners and in public places'. By a room he means a place that is secluded from the tumult and sight of the world, where prayer can be offered more purely and quietly, such as the seclusion of monastic solitude, a place where we are told to shut the door, that is, to close up every approach, lest something happen to hinder the purity of prayer and what we see distract the unfortunate soul.

Yet there are many wearing our habit who despise this counsel, or rather, this divine precept, and we find them hard to tolerate when they celebrate the divine offices with cloister or choir wide open and conduct themselves shamelessly in full view of both men and women, especially during the Mass when they are decked out in precious ornaments like those of the worldly men to whom they display them. In their view a feast is best celebrated if it is rich in external display and lavish in food and drink. Better to keep silence, as it is shameful to speak of their wretched blindness that is wholly contrary to the religion of Christ's poor. At heart they are like Jews, following their own custom instead of a rule, making a mockery of God's command in their practices, looking to usage, not duty; although, as St Augustine reminds us, the Lord said, 'I am truth' not 'I am custom.' Anyone who cares to may entrust himself to the prayers of these men, which are offered with doors open, but you who have been led by the king of heaven himself into his chamber and rest in his embrace, and with the door always shut are wholly given up to him, are more intimately joined to him, in the Apostle's words, 'But anyone who is joined to the Lord is one spirit with him.' So much the more confidence, then, have I in the purity and effectiveness of your prayers, and the more urgently I demand your help. And I believe these prayers are offered more devoutly on my behalf because we are bound together in such great mutual love.

But if I have distressed you by mentioning the dangers which beset me or the death I fear, it was done in accordance with your own request, or rather, entreaty. For the first letter you wrote me has a passage which says:

And so in the name of Christ, who is still giving you some protection for his service, we beseech you to write as often as you think fit to us who are his handmaids and yours, with news of the perils in which you are still storm-tossed. We are all that are left you, so at least you should let us share your sorrow or your joy. It is always some consolation in sorrow to feel that it is shared, and any burden laid on several is carried more lightly or removed.

Why then do you accuse me of making you share my anxiety when I was forced to do so at your own behest? When I am suffering in despair of my life, would it be fitting for you to be joyous? Would you want to be partners only in joy, not grief, to join in rejoicing without weeping with those who weep? There is no wider distinction between true friends and false than the fact that the former share adversity, the latter only prosperity.

Say no more, I beg you, and cease from complaints like these which are so far removed from the true depths of love! Yet even if you are still offended by this, I am so critically placed in danger and daily despair of life that it is proper for me to take thought for the welfare of my soul, and to provide for it while I may. Nor will you, if you truly love me, take exception to my forethought. Indeed, had you any hope of divine mercy being shown me, you would be all the more anxious for me to be freed from the troubles of this life as you see them to be intolerable. At least you must know that whoever frees me from life will deliver me from the greatest suffering. What I may afterwards incur is uncertain, but from what I shall be set free is not in question. Every unhappy life is happy in its ending, and those who feel true sympathy and pain for the anxieties of others want to see these ended, even to their own loss, if they really love those they see suffer and think more of their friends' advantage than of their own. So when a son has long been ill a mother wants his illness to end even in death, for she finds it unbearable, and can more easily face bereavement than have him share her misery. And anyone who takes special pleasure in the presence of a friend would rather have him happy in absence than present and unhappy, for he finds suffering intolerable if he cannot relieve it. In your case, you are not even permitted to enjoy my presence, unhappy though it is, and so, when any provision you are able to make for me is to your own advantage, I cannot see why you should prefer me to live on in great misery rather than be happier in death. If you see your advantage in prolonging my miseries, you are proved an enemy rather than a friend. But if you hesitate to appear in such a guise, I beg you, as I said before, to cease your complaints.

However, I approve of your rejection of praise, for

in this very thing you show yourself more praiseworthy. It is written that 'He who is first in accusing himself is just' and 'Whoever humbles himself will be exalted.' May your written words be reflected in your heart! If they are, yours is true humility and will not vanish with anything I say. But be careful, I beg you, not to seek praise when you appear to shun it, and not to reject with your lips what you desire in your heart. St Jerome writes to the virgin Eustochium on this point, amongst others: 'We are led on by our natural evil. We give willing ear to our flatterers, and though we may answer that we are unworthy and an artful blush suffuses our cheeks, the soul inwardly delights in its own praise.' Such artfulness Virgil describes in the wanton Galatea, who sought what she wanted by flight, and by feigning rejection led on her lover more surely towards her:

She flees to the willows and wishes first to be seen.

Before she hides she wants to be seen fleeing, so that the very flight whereby she appears to reject the youth's company ensures that she obtains it. Similarly, when we seem to shun men's praise we are directing it towards ourselves, and when we pretend that we wish to hide lest anyone discovers what to praise in us, we are leading the unwary on to give us praise because in this way we appear to deserve it. I mention this because it is a common occurrence, not because I suspect such things of you; I have no doubts about your humility. But I want you to refrain from speaking like this, so that you do not appear to those who do not know you so well to be seeking fame by shunning it, as Jerome says. My praise will never make you proud, but will summon you to higher things, and the more eager you are to please me, the more anxious you will be to embrace what I praise. My praise is not a tribute to your piety which is intended to bolster up your pride, and we ought not in fact to believe in our friends' approval any more than in our enemies' abuse.

I come at last to your old perpetual complaint, as we have called it, in which you presume to blame God for the manner of our entry into religion instead of wishing to glorify him as you justly should. I had thought that this bitterness of heart at what was so clear an act of divine mercy had long since disappeared. The more dangerous such bitterness is to you in wearing out body and soul alike, the more pitiful it is and distressing to me. If you are anxious to please me in everything, as you claim, and in this at least would end my torment, or even give me the greatest pleasure, you must rid yourself of it. If it persists you can neither please me nor attain bliss with me. Can you bear me to come to this without you – I whom you declare yourself ready to follow to the very fires of hell? Seek piety in this at least, lest you cut yourself off from me who am hastening, you believe, towards God; be the readier to do so because the goal we must come to will be blessed, and our companionship the more welcome for being happier. Remember what you have said, recall what you have written, namely that in the manner of our conversion, when God seems to have been more my adversary, he has clearly shown himself kinder. For this reason at least you must accept his will, that it is most salutary for me, and for you too, if your transports of grief will see reason. You should not grieve because you are the cause of so great a good, for which you must not doubt you were specially created by God. Nor should you weep because I have to bear this, except when our blessings through the martyrs in their sufferings and the Lord's death sadden you. If it had befallen me justly, would you find it easier to bear? Would it distress you less? In fact if it had been so, the result would have been greater disgrace for me and more credit to my enemies, since justice would have won them approval while my guilt would have brought me into contempt. And no one would be stirred by pity for me to condemn what was done.

However, it may relieve the bitterness of your grief if I prove that this came upon us justly, as well as to our advantage, and that God's punishment was more properly directed against us when we were married than when we were living in sin. After our marriage, when you were living in the cloister with the nuns at Argenteuil and I came one day to visit you privately, you know what my uncontrollable desire did with you there, actually in a corner of the refectory, since we had nowhere else to go. I repeat, you know how shamelessly we behaved on that occasion in so hallowed a place, dedicated to the most holy Virgin. Even if our other shameful behaviour was ended, this alone would deserve far heavier punishment. Need I recall our previous fornication and the wanton impurities which preceded our marriage, or my supreme act of betrayal, when I deceived your uncle about you so disgracefully, at a time when I was continuously living with him in his own house? Who would not judge me justly betrayed by the man whom I had first shamelessly betrayed? Do you think that the momentary pain of that wound is sufficient punishment for such crimes? Or rather, that so great an advantage was fitting for such great wickedness? What wound do you suppose would satisfy God's justice for the profanation such as I described of a place so sacred to his own Mother? Surely, unless I am much mistaken, not that wound which was wholly beneficial was intended as a punishment for this, but rather the daily unending torment I now endure.

You know too how when you were pregnant and I took you to my own country you disguised yourself in the sacred habit of a nun, a pretence which was an irreverent mockery of the religion you now profess. Consider, then, how fittingly divine justice, or rather, divine grace brought you against your will to the religion which you did not hesitate to mock, so that you should willingly expiate your profanation in the same habit, and the truth of reality should remedy the lie of your pretence and correct your falsity. And if you would allow consideration of our advantage to be an element in divine justice, you would be able to call what God did to us then an act not of justice, but of grace.

See then, my beloved, see how with the dragnets of his mercy the Lord has fished us up from the depth of this dangerous sea, and from the abyss of what a Charybdis he has saved our shipwrecked selves, although we were unwilling, so that each of us may justly break out in that cry: 'The Lord takes thought for me.' Think and think again of the great perils in which we were and from which the Lord rescued us; tell always with the deepest gratitude how much the Lord has done for our souls. Comfort by our example any unrighteous who despair of God's goodness, so that all may know what may be done for those who ask with prayer, when such benefits are granted sinners even against their will. Consider the magnanimous design of God's mercy for us, the compassion with which the Lord directed his judgement towards our chastisement, the wisdom whereby he made use of evil itself and mercifully set aside our impiety, so that by a wholly justified wound in a single part of my body he might heal two souls. Compare our danger and manner of deliverance, compare the sickness and the medicine. Examine the cause, our deserts, and marvel at the effect, his pity.

You know the depths of shame to which my unbridled lust had consigned our bodies, until no reverence for decency or for God even during the days of Our Lord's Passion, or of the greater sacraments could keep me from wallowing in this mire. Even when you were unwilling, resisted to the utmost of your power and tried to dissuade me, as yours was the weaker nature I often forced you to consent with threats and blows. So intense were the fires of lust which bound me to you that I set those wretched, obscene pleasures, which we blush even to name, above God as above myself; nor would it seem that divine mercy could have taken action except by forbidding me these pleasures altogether, without future hope. And so it was wholly just and merciful, although by means of the supreme treachery of your uncle, for me to be reduced in that part of my body which was the seat of lust and sole reason for those desires, so that I could increase in many ways; in order that this member should justly be punished for all its wrongdoing in us, expiate in suffering the sins committed for its amusement and cut me off from the slough of filth in which I had been wholly immersed in mind as in body. Only thus could I become more fit to approach the holy altars, now that no contagion of carnal impurity would ever again call me from them. How mercifully did he want me to suffer so much only in that member, the privation of which would also further the salvation of my soul without defiling my body nor preventing any performance of my duties! Indeed, it would make me readier to perform whatever can be honourably done by setting me wholly free from the heavy yoke of carnal desire.

So when divine grace cleansed rather than deprived me of those vilest members which from their practice of utmost indecency are called 'the parts of shame' and have no proper name of their own, what else did it do but remove a foul imperfection in order to preserve perfect purity? Such purity, as we have heard, certain sages have desired so eagerly that they have mutilated themselves, so as to remove entirely the shame of desire. The Apostle too is recorded as having besought the Lord to rid him of this thorn in the flesh, but was not heard. The great Christian philosopher Origen provides an example, for he was not afraid to mutilate himself in order to quench completely this fire within him, as if he understood literally the words that those men were truly blessed who castrated themselves for the Kingdom of Heaven's sake, and believed them to be truthfully carrying out the bidding of the Lord about offending members, that we should cut them off and throw them away; and as if he interpreted as historic fact, not as a hidden symbol, that prophecy of Isaiah in which the Lord prefers eunuchs to the rest of the faithful: 'The eunuchs who keep my sabbaths, and choose to do my will I will give a place in my own house and within my walls and a name better than sons and daughters. I will give them an everlasting name which shall not perish.' Yet Origen is seriously to be blamed because he sought a remedy for blame in punishment of his body. True, he has zeal for God, but an ill-informed zeal, and the charge of homicide can be made against him for his self-mutilation. People think he did this either at the suggestion of the devil or in grave error but, in my case, through God's compassion, it was done by another's hand. I do not incur blame, I escape it. I deserve death and gain life. I am summoned and reprieved; I persist in crime and am pardoned against my will. The Apostle prays and is not heard, he persists in prayer and is not answered. Truly the Lord takes thought for me. I will go then and declare how much the Lord has done for my soul.

Come too, my inseparable companion, and join me in thanksgiving, you who were made my partner both in guilt and in grace. For the Lord is not unmindful also of your own salvation, indeed, he has you much in mind, for by a kind of holy presage of his name he marked you out to be especially his when he named you Heloise, after his own name, Elohim. In his mercy, I say, he intended to provide for two people in one, the two whom the devil sought to destroy in one; since a short while before this happening he had bound us together by the indissoluble bond of the marriage sacrament. At the time I desired to keep you whom I loved beyond measure for myself alone for ever, but he was already planning to use this opportunity for our joint conversion to himself. Had you not been previously joined to me in wedlock, you might easily have clung to the world when I withdrew from it, either at the suggestion of your relatives or in enjoyment of carnal delights. See then, how greatly the Lord was concerned for us, as if he were reserving us for some great ends, and was indignant or grieved because our knowledge of letters, the talents which he had entrusted to us, were not being used to glorify his name; or as if he feared for his humble and incontinent servant, because it is written 'Women make even the wise forsake their faith.' Indeed, this is proved in the case of the wisest of men, Solomon.

How great an interest the talent of your own wisdom pays daily to the Lord in the many spiritual daughters you have born for him, while I remain totally barren and labour in vain amongst the sons of perdition! What a hateful loss and grievous misfortune if you had abandoned yourself to the defilement of carnal pleasures only to bear in suffering a few children for the world, when now you are delivered in exultation of numerous progeny for heaven! Nor would you have been more than a woman, whereas now you rise even above men, and have turned the curse of Eve into the blessing of Mary. How unseemly for those holy hands which now turn the pages of sacred books to have to do the obscene degradations of women's work! God himself has thought fit to raise us up from the contamination of this filth and the pleasures of this mire and draw us to him by force – the same force whereby he chose to strike and convert Paul – and by our example perhaps to deter from our audacity others who are also trained in letters.

I beg you then, sister, do not be aggrieved, do not vex the Father who corrects us in fatherly wise; pay heed to what is written: 'Whom the Lord loves he reproves' and 'He lays the rod on every son whom he acknowledges.' And elsewhere: 'A father who spares the rod hates his son.' This punishment is momentary, not eternal, and for our purification, not damnation. Hear the prophet and take heart: 'The Lord will not judge twice on the same issue and no second tribulation shall arise.' Listen too to that supreme and mighty exhortation of the Truth: 'By your endurance you will possess your souls.' Solomon, too: 'Better be slow to anger than be a fighter; and master one's heart rather than storm a city.' Are you not moved to tears or remorse by the only begotten Son of God who, for you and for all mankind, in his innocence was seized by the hands of impious men, dragged along and scourged, blindfolded, mocked at, buffeted, spat upon, crowned with thorns, finally hanged between thieves on the Cross, at the time so shameful a gibbet, to die a horrible and accursed form of death? Have this man always, sister, as your true spouse and the spouse of all the Church. Keep him in mind. Look at him going to be crucified for your sake, carrying his own cross. Be one of the crowd, one of the women who wept and lamented over him, as Luke tells: 'A great crowd of people followed, many women among them, who wept and lamented over him.' To these he graciously turned and mercifully foretold the destruction which would come to avenge his death, against which they could provide, if they understood. 'Daughters of Jerusalem,' he said, 'do not weep for me; no, weep for yourselves and your children. For the days are surely coming when they will say, "Happy are the barren, the wombs that never bore a child, the breasts that never fed one." Then they will start saying to the mountains, "Fall on us," and to the hills, "Cover us." For if these things are done when the wood is green, what will happen when it is dry?'

Have compassion on him who suffered willingly for your redemption, and look with remorse on him who was crucified for you. In your mind be always present at his tomb, weep and wail with the faithful women, of whom it is written, as I said, 'The women sitting at the tomb wept and lamented for the Lord.' Prepare with them the perfumes for his burial, but better perfumes, which are of the spirit, not of the body, for this is the fragrance he needs though he rejected the other. Be remorseful over this with all your powers of devotion, for he exhorts the faithful to this remorse and compassion in the words of Jeremiah: 'All you who pass by, look and see if there is any sorrow like my sorrow.' That is, if there is some sufferer for whom you should sorrow in compassion when I alone, for no guilt of mine, atone for the sins of others. He himself is the way whereby the faithful pass from exile to their own country. He too has set up the Cross, from which he summons us, as a ladder for us to use. On this, for you, the only begotten Son of God was killed; he was made an offering because he wished it. Grieve with compassion over him alone and share his suffering in your grief. Fulfil what was foretold of devout souls through the prophet Zachariah: 'They shall wail for him as over an only child, and shall grieve for him as for the death of a first-born son.'

See, sister, what great mourning there is amongst those who love their king over the death of his only and first begotten son. Behold the lamentation and grief with which the whole household and court are consumed; and when you come to the bride of the only son who is dead, you will find her wailing intolerable and more than you can bear. This mourning, sister, should be yours and also the wailing, for you were joined to one in Christ, one flesh according to the law of matrimony. Whatever is yours cannot, I think, fail to be mine, and Christ is yours because you have become his bride. Now, as I said before, you have as a servant me whom in the past you recognized as your lord, more your own now when bound to you by spiritual love than one subjected by fear. And so I have

increasing confidence that you will plead for us both
before him and, through your prayer, I may be granted
what I cannot obtain through my own; especially now,
when the daily pressure of dangers and disturbances
threaten my life and give me no time for prayer. Nor
can I imitate that blessed eunuch, the high official of
Candace, Queen of Ethiopia, who had charge of all
her wealth, and had come from so far to worship in
Jerusalem. He was on his way home when the apostle
Philip was sent by the angel to convert him to the
faith, as he had already deserved by his prayers and his
assiduous reading of the Scriptures. Because he did
not want to take time from this even on his journey,
although he was a man of great wealth and a gentile,
it came about through the great goodness of providence
that the passage of Scripture was before him which gave
the apostle the perfect opportunity for his conversion.

So that nothing may delay my petition nor defer its
fulfilment, I hasten to compose and send to you this
prayer, which you may offer to the Lord in supplication
on our behalf:

God, who at the beginning of human creation, in forming
woman from a rib of man didst especially sanctify the sacrament of the marriage bond, and who didst glorify marriage
with boundless honours both by being born of one given in
marriage and by the first of thy miracles; thou who moreover
didst grant this remedy for the incontinence of my frailty,
in such manner as pleased thee, despise not the prayers of
thy humble handmaid which I pour out as a suppliant in the
presence of thy majesty for my own excesses and those

of my beloved. Pardon, O most gracious, who art rather graciousness itself, pardon our many great offences, and let the ineffable immensity of thy mercy test the multitude of our faults. Punish the guilty now, I beseech thee, that thou mayst spare them hereafter. Punish now, lest thou punish in eternity. Take to thy servants the rod of correction, not the sword of wrath. Afflict their flesh that thou mayst preserve their souls. Come as a redeemer, not an avenger; gracious rather than just; the merciful Father, not the stern Lord. Prove us, Lord, and test us, in the manner in which the prophet asks for himself, as if he said openly: First consider my strength and measure accordingly the burden of my testing. This is what St Paul promises to the faithful, when he says 'God keeps faith, and he will not allow you to be tested beyond your powers, but when the test comes he will also provide a way out, so that you are able to sustain it.' Thou hast joined us, Lord, and thou hast parted us, when and in what manner it pleased thee. Now, Lord, what thou hast mercifully begun, most mercifully end, and those whom thou hast parted for a time on earth, unite forever to thyself in heaven: thou who art our hope, our portion, our expectation and our consolation, O Lord, who art blessed world without end. Amen.

Farewell in Christ, bride of Christ; in Christ fare well and live in Christ.

THE STORY OF PENGUIN CLASSICS

Before 1946 ... 'Classics' are mainly the domain of academics and students, without readable editions for everyone else. This all changes when a little-known classicist, E. V. Rieu, presents Penguin founder Allen Lane with the translation of Homer's Odyssey that he has been working on and reading to his wife Nelly in his spare time.

1946 The Odyssey becomes the first Penguin Classic published, and promptly sells three million copies. Suddenly, classic books are no longer for the privileged few.

1950s Rieu, now series editor, turns to professional writers for the best modern, readable translations, including Dorothy L. Sayers's *Inferno* and Robert Graves's *The Twelve Caesars*, which revives the salacious original.

1960s 1961 sees the arrival of the Penguin Modern Classics, showcasing the best twentieth-century writers from around the world. Rieu retires in 1964, hailing the Penguin Classics list as 'the greatest educative force of the 20th century'.

1970s A new generation of translators arrives to swell the Penguin Classics ranks, and the list grows to encompass more philosophy, religion, science, history and politics.

1980s The Penguin American Library joins the Classics stable, with titles such as *The Last of the Mohicans* safeguarded. Penguin Classics now offers the most comprehensive library of world literature available.

1990s Penguin Popular Classics are launched, offering readers budget editions of the greatest works of literature. Penguin Audiobooks brings the classics to a listening audience for the first time, and in 1999 the launch of the Penguin Classics website takes them online to an ever larger global readership.

The 21st Century Penguin Classics are rejacketed for the first time in nearly twenty years. This world famous series now consists of more than 1,300 titles, making the widest range of the best books ever written available to millions – and constantly redefining the meaning of what makes a 'classic'.

The Odyssey continues ...

The best books ever written

PENGUIN (P) CLASSICS

SINCE 1946